# A Graphically Illustrated Kindle Fire HD 8 Guide

Pam Padgett

Joan Boney

ISBN: 1530316804
ISBN-13: 978-1530316809

# TABLE OF CONTENTS

PREFACE: CASE STUDIES ........................................................................................ 7

1. INITIAL SETUP .................................................................................................. 9

CHARGING THE BATTERY .......................................................................... 9
TOP EDGE OF UNIT ................................................................................. 10
INSTALLATION BEGINS ............................................................................ 11
WALLPAPER (SCREEN BACKGROUND) ...................................................... 13
THE CAMERA ICON ON COVER PAGE ...................................................... 13
UNLOCKING THE COVER PAGE ................................................................ 14
SETTING UP EMAIL ................................................................................. 14
SLIPPERY SURFACE OF UNIT ................................................................... 16

2. HOME PAGE SCREEN ..................................................................................... 19

MEANING OF EACH SYMBOL ON HOME SCREEN ....................................... 19
NAME OF DEVICE: (CHANGING DEVICE NAME) ........................................ 20
WI-FI EMBLEM ........................................................................................ 22
BATTERY STRENGTH ............................................................................... 23
TIME OF DAY .......................................................................................... 23
THE "SEARCH BOX" ON HOME SCREEN ................................................... 26
THE "CAROUSEL": HOME / BOOKS & MORE .............................................. 27
LIBRARY: APPS THAT ARE DOWNLOADED ............................................... 29
ICONS ON HOME SCREEN: HIGHWAYS .................................................... 31

3. THE HOME PAGE: EVERYTHING BEGINS HERE ............................................. 33

THE NON-COMPUTER GENERATIONS ........................................................ 33
HIGHWAYS .............................................................................................. 34
HOME IS THE CENTER OF EVERYTHING ................................................... 36
PRACTICING: HOME PAGE TO EACH ICON ............................................... 37
YOUR FIRST SHOPPING TRIP ................................................................... 38
GETTING FROM HOME TO THE INTERNET ................................................. 44
ALL HIGHWAYS START AT YOUR HOME PAGE .......................................... 45
EVERYTHING BEGINS / ENDS AT HOME PAGE .......................................... 46

4. SETTINGS: 1 ................................................................................................... 49

BRIGHTNESS OF SCREEN ......................................................................... 49
ADJUSTING SIZE OF PRINT ...................................................................... 51
    *Books:* ............................................................................................... 51
    *Internet:* ............................................................................................ 52
    *Emails:* .............................................................................................. 56
SCREEN ROTATION (VERTICAL / HORIZONTAL) ......................................... 60

**5. SETTINGS: 2**..........................................................................**65**

NOTIFICATION OF ARRIVING EMAILS .......................................65

BOOKS: FONTS, SCREEN COLOR, MARGINS, LINE SPACING ...........68

KEYBOARDS...........................................................................72

**6. MOVING ICONS / SETTING WALLPAPER** ................................**77**

TO MOVE AN ICON..................................................................77

CREATING A FILE OF ICONS....................................................78

WARNING ABOUT REMOVING ICONS .......................................80

WALLPAPER (SCREEN BACKGROUND).......................................82

**7. EMAIL CONTACTS: CREATE A CONTACT** ..............................**85**

FROM AN ADDRESS INSIDE AN EMAIL ......................................85

MANUALLY: FROM EMAIL ADDRESS (WITH NO EMAIL) ..............91

**8. EMAIL CONTACTS: EDITING / SETTINGS FAVORITES**............**95**

EDIT A CONTACT....................................................................95

SET A CONTACT AS "FAVORITE" ............................................99

**9. EMAILS: VIEWING, REPLYING TO, AND FORWARDING**............**103**

THE INBOX SCREEN...............................................................103

REPLY TO AN EMAIL ............................................................105

FORWARD AN EMAIL.............................................................107

REFRESH INBOX (BRING IN NEW EMAILS) ..............................110

**10. EMAILS: CREATING AND DELETING**................................**113**

CREATE AN EMAIL ...............................................................113

DELETE EMAIL YOU ARE VIEWING ........................................118

DELETE MULTIPLE EMAILS....................................................119

DELETE EMAILS ONE AT A TIME FROM INBOX.........................120

**11. BOOKS** ........................................................................**121**

ORDER BOOK FROM AMAZON SHOP .......................................121

BOOKMARKS.........................................................................125

REMOVE BOOK FROM YOUR ACTIVE LIBRARY .........................128

RETRIEVE BOOK FROM STORAGE AND RETURN TO LIBRARY .......132

**12. INTERNET**....................................................................**135**

USE SEARCH TO GET TO A WEB-SITE .....................................137

BOOKMARKS.........................................................................140

CREATE MULTIPLE TABS (SWITCHING BETWEEN INTERNET SITES)....143

SETTING THE DEFAULT SEARCH ENGINE .................................147

REFRESHING THE SCREEN (TO SEE CURRENT INFORMATION) .......151

REMOVING A TAB..................................................................152

**13. PLAYING INTERNET RADIO THROUGH KINDLE** .................................. 153

Public Radio Stations (free to listener) ................................. 153
Loading The "TuneIn" App ........................................................ 153
Bringing In Music After App Is Installed ................................. 159

**14. AMAZON PRIME: MUSIC, VIDEO, BOOKS** ...................................... 163

Introduction To Amazon Prime ................................................. 163

**15. MUSIC: CATEGORIES** ................................................................ 167

Recent Activities, Prime Music, Library ................................. 167
Finding Main Menu ................................................................... 170
To Get From Music Screen Back To Main Menu ....................... 171

**16. MUSIC: COMPOSITIONS** ........................................................... 173

Downloading Music .................................................................. 173
To Locate Downloaded Music ................................................... 176
Excellence Of Classical Music Selections ................................. 177

**17. MUSIC: LOCATIONS** ................................................................ 179

Recent Activities Category ........................................................ 179
Prime Music Category ............................................................... 184
Library (Cloud Library) Category .............................................. 188
To Create A Playlist .................................................................. 189

**18. TV STREAMING** ....................................................................... 195

Locating The Streamer .............................................................. 196
To Obtain The App .................................................................... 199

**19. CAMERA** ................................................................................. 203

Taking Pictures With Kindle Camera ........................................ 203
Using The Front-Facing Camera ............................................... 207
Camera Settings ........................................................................ 208
Viewing Photos ......................................................................... 210
Editing A Photo ......................................................................... 215
Email Photos ............................................................................. 218
Deleting Photos ......................................................................... 223

**20. SCREEN PRINTS: REPRODUCTION OF KINDLE SCREEN** ............ 227

Create A Screen Print ............................................................... 227
Email A Screen Print ................................................................ 228

**21. MICROPHONE: DICTATION ON KINDLE** .................................. 231

Practice Using The Microphone ............................................... 234

**22. REBOOTING ... CORRECTING PROBLEMS** ....................... 235

**23. REMOVING ADVERTISEMENTS** ............................... 239

**24. DEREGISTERING KINDLE** ................................... 245

**A LIGHTER TOUCH FOR ANIMAL LOVERS** ....................... 253

**SPECIAL TREATS ... REBOOTING HUMANS** ..................... 261

**MORE** ...................................................... 271

# Preface:  Case Studies

*This guide is written for people who **have little or no experience operating a computer**.*

*The goal is to provide a step by step plan for the reader **to have success** in operating a Kindle Fire (5th generation) and to experience the many joys and helps that come from this magnificent device.*

**One 77-year-old man was in our test group**
using this book to learn to use the Kindle.  He is confined to wheelchair after a very serious heart operation.  One hand ended up partially paralyzed and he reported he was having difficulty lifting his paper Bible.   He had very limited experience with a computer.  His wife reported the following:
"John is very impressed.  He can understand everything as we go along and the pictures of each step are a life saver.  What a wonderful concept."

**One of our test group is an 80-year-old woman**
who has many physical handicaps, walks with a walker, and her 94-year-old husband died a few weeks before she began trying to learn to use the Kindle.  She took this book and used it to teach

herself the basic principles.  <u>It provided valuable therapy for her in a serious time of adjustment.</u>  It helped occupy her mind and gave her <u>a new mental project.</u>  One of our authors called her almost daily for the first month and coached her.  The author lives in Colorado and this woman is life-long New Yorker (NYC).  She is really doing well in using the Kindle.  **Can you imagine how much this can mean to her?**

**This is exactly why we compiled this material ... to help people, especially older people and physically handicapped people, who are confined to one physical space (wheelchair / bed).  This gives each person an opportunity to get books and read books without going to library or book store.  This device stores music, books, video in a unit which can be held in the hand and should be easily within reach of confined individuals.  It helps each of us pass time and even enjoy time on this present earth in difficult periods of life.  All we have to do is learn to use it.  <u>And we can</u>!**

<u>**CREATED  BY**</u>:
Pam Padgett
Joan Boney

<u>**ON  COVER:**</u>
Building Blocks by Kid Kraft
60 PC Wooden Block Set  (available on amazon.com)

# 1. Initial Setup

## Charging The Battery

**Remove battery cable from box.**

Plug into top edge of Kindle and electrical outlet on wall to fully charge the unit.

| Volume controls (2 silver bars) | EarPhone Input | Battery/ Charger | On/Off (1 silver bar) |
| --- | --- | --- | --- |

**(Note: On top of one side of the plug that goes into the Kindle, <u>you will see a small design</u>. This is the up side of the plug. You might put a white sticker on this side of plug to help you see up side. You cannot reverse the direction. Up is toward the face of the screen when the cable is plugged into the battery charge outlet.)**

## When battery charge gets low, screen will look similar to following:

**Short battery cord:**  The battery recharge cord that comes with the Kindle is very short.  What I do is use an extension cord, putting the extension cord into wall outlet and plugging the Kindle into the extension cord.  This allows me to use the Kindle from my recliner while the battery is recharging.

## Top Edge Of Unit

To turn the unit <u>on/off</u>:  ***press/release*** on the single silver bar on right top edge of Kindle.

| Volume controls (2 silver bars) | EarPhone Input | Battery/ Charger | On/Off (1 silver bar) |
|---|---|---|---|

## Installation Begins

When you plug in your Kindle for the first time and press the On/Off button, you will see a message letting you know that your Kindle is starting. After this the screen may be completely black for a few seconds. **Don't panic**.

**Before long installation information will appear on screen.** Installation is very easy to do. Just follow the directions as they appear on the screen. There are several steps involved.

You will need to have **the name of your wi-fi network** and **your wi-fi password** in order to connect to the internet during installation.

You will also need to have **your Amazon login and password** so you can register your Kindle during the installation process.

**During installation you will often see the word "installing" (or downloading) and a yellow line under that word will show you the progress of the installation and when it is finished the yellow line disappears and the next step will begin for the initiating of the start-up.**

**You are given the option not to choose a start-up password. If you choose a password, <u>each time you turn on unit</u> you will be required to enter a password.** *(I did not choose password for I don't need one for the way I use my Kindle.)*

After you have completed the installation process, the Cover Page ("lock screen") will be on screen:

## Wallpaper (Screen Background)

**A background picture (called Wallpaper) appears on screen.**

*In a few seconds the screen will begin to dim. To make the screen brighter again, tap one time on face of the screen.*

## The Camera Icon On Cover Page

The camera icon in the extreme bottom right corner of the Cover screen allows you to take a picture from the Cover screen. Later you can use a photo as the **"wallpaper"** *(background on the screen)* for your cover page and home page.

*(Changing wallpaper is optional.)*

# Unlocking The Cover Page

The **"lock"** symbol at the bottom center of the cover page is to unlock the cover page and take you to the home page. Put your finger on the "lock" icon and hold finger down and "swipe" (drag) your finger upward. You'll see a new screen called the Home Page.

# Setting Up Email

This is a good time to setup your Kindle to send and receive emails. **You will need your email address and email password to do this.**

From the Home screen tap on the Email icon:

A screen will come up with a place for you to type in your email address. Tap on that line and a keyboard will come up at the bottom of the screen. **Type in your email address, then tap the button labeled "Next".**

Another screen will come up with a place for you to type in your email password. **Type in your email password, then tap the button labeled "Next".**

After your email address and password have been verified, you will see a screen letting you know your email setup is complete.

You can return to the Home screen with one tap on the circle at the bottom of the screen:

# Slippery Surface Of Unit

**While the unit is very attractive in appearance, it is a little slippery due to the slick finish**.  I took electrical tape and cut small strips of tape *(approximately 4 inches long)* and spaced these strips at intervals along the back.

## Picture #1

<u>**Picture #1**</u> shows the back of a unit with **black electrical tape** on the top, bottom, and sides of the back of the unit.  As you can see from this

picture, you can't see the electrical tape when the tape is black. *(In real life, you can see the tape if you look closely at the back of the Kindle but it isn't very noticeable.)* If you cut the strips carefully and curve the ends as you cut the tape, it seems better to me.

Camera Eye

## Picture #2

**Picture #2** has masking tape over the electrical tape so you can see approximately where I placed the black electrical tape on the unit.

**Be careful on back of unit not to cover the camera eye located on one back corner.**

These strips of **black** electrical tape provide just enough traction to make the unit secure in my hand. It only took single strips of tape to accomplish this. **Be careful not to cover the 2 speaker outlets on one side of the unit.** Keep the strips on the back of the unit and do not allow them to lap over onto the sides.

**If you decide to remove the electrical tape**, it will not damage the surface. I used an eyeglass wipe cloth to clean the surface when removing the electrical tape.

**The first time I did this to the Kindle, I covered the entire back with electrical tape.** Later I realized I did not need the tape to cover the complete back side of the Kindle. All I really needed was the tape to go at intervals around the back of unit as you see can see in **Picture #2**.

# 2. Home Page Screen

## Meaning of Each Symbol on Home Screen

When you receive your Kindle, the **Home Page** screen will look similar to this:

# Name Of Device: (Changing Device Name)

At the top left-hand corner of the screen shown on the previous page, you will see "Pam's 8" (5th generation Fire)", the name of this device. **This name may be changed if you wish to do so.**

On the Home screen, tap on the **Settings** icon ...

Another screen comes up.

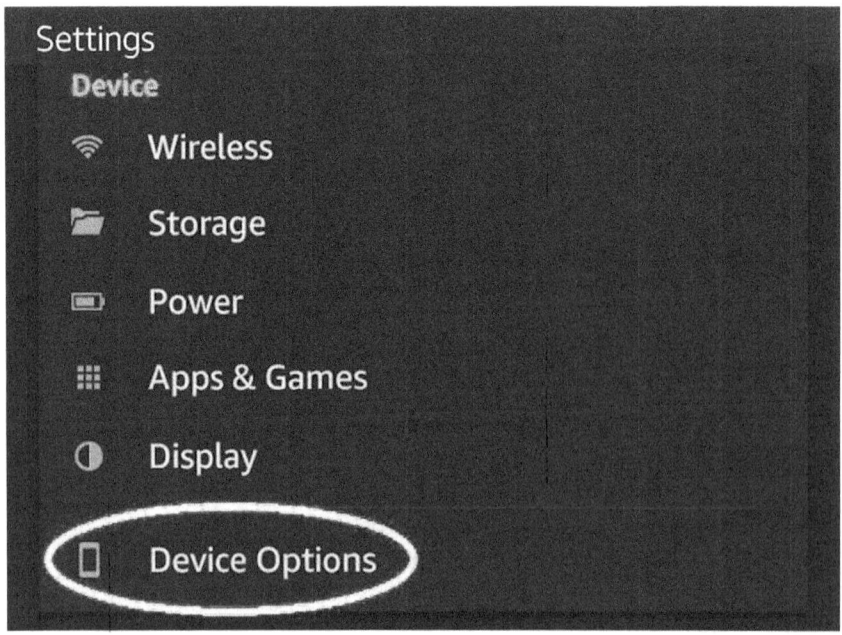

## Tap on:  Device Options.

You'll see ...

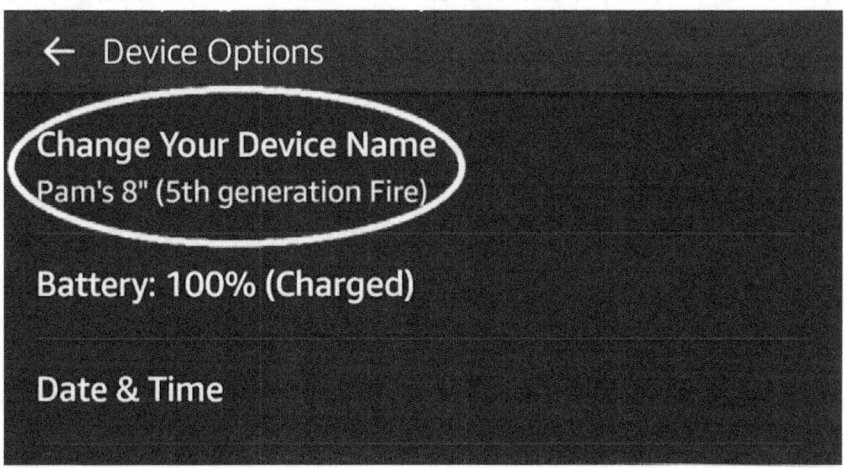

## Tap on:  Change Your Device Name

Another screen appears:

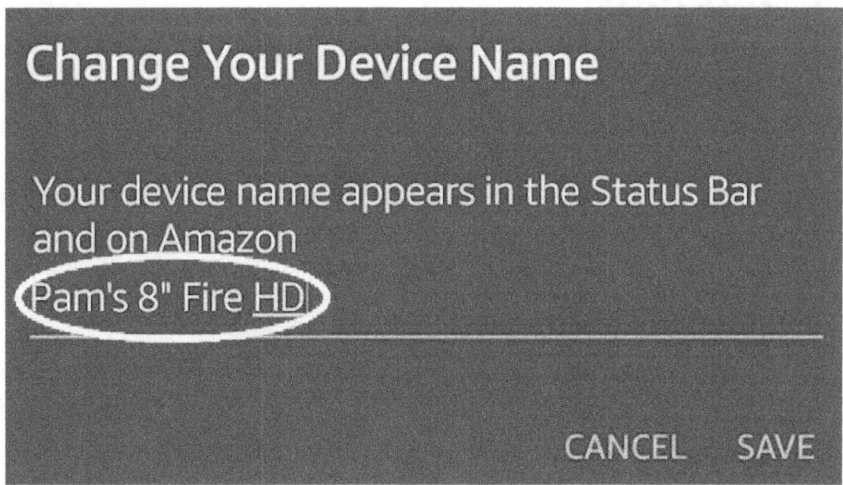

Use the Delete key on the keyboard ![delete key] to back space.  Each time you tap this key on keyboard,  a letter of the device name will be deleted.  After you delete the name of the device, type in the name you have chosen for this device.

After you have typed in the name you want, tap **SAVE**

Return to HOME PAGE by **one tap on the circle at the bottom of the screen.**

## Wi-Fi Emblem

This emblem ▨ at top of the Kindle screen is an emblem for "Wi-Fi". It shows you how strong your Wi-Fi is with fully lighted emblem being strongest strength.

# Battery Strength

The % of battery strength remaining in the Kindle is shown at top of page:

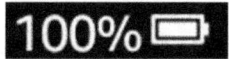

# Time Of Day

At the top right-hand corner of the screen you will see the time of day.  If your device shows the time in 24-hour format (military time) such as 22:53, you can change this if you wish.

Tap on the **Settings** icon from the Home screen:

# The Settings screen comes up.

## Tap on:  Device Options

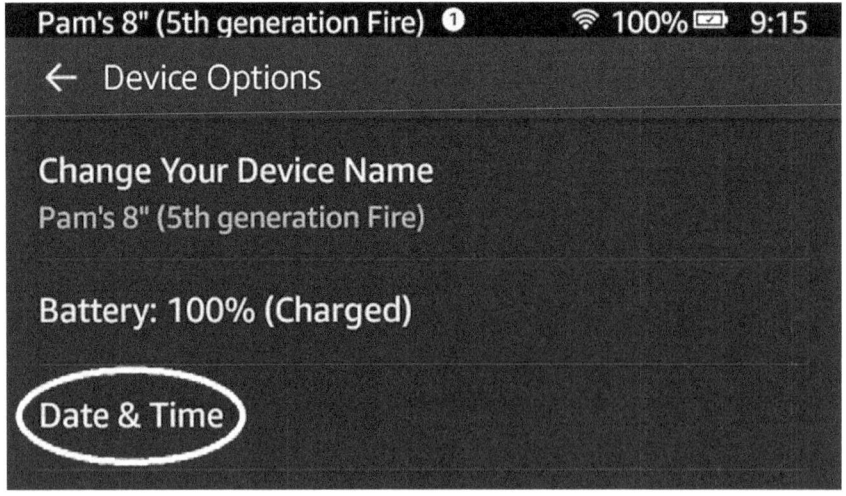

## Tap on:  Date & Time

The following screen comes up ...

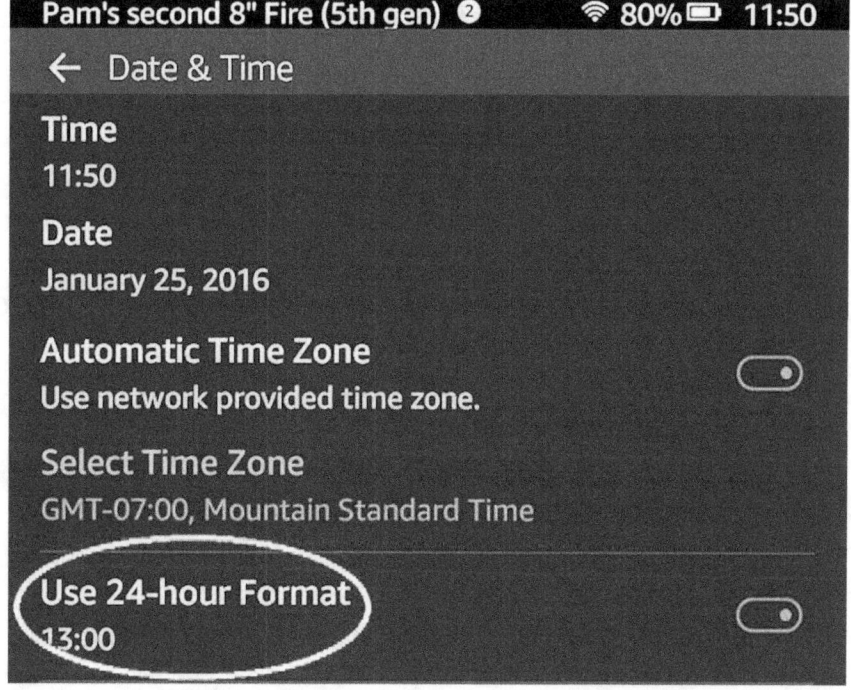

**Use 24 hour Format**:  The gold colored oval (switch) on the right side of the screen indicates that military time is set.

Tap the gold oval (switch) to set non-military time.  The oval (switch) turns gray in color.

You can now go back to the Home screen by one tap on the circle at the bottom of the screen.

# The "Search Box" On Home Screen

On HOME PAGE there is **a search box** at top of screen, where you can initiate **a search**.

Tap in the search box and a keyboard will come up at the bottom of the screen.

Type your search request into the search box, then tap on the yellow circle in the bottom right corner of the keyboard.

# The "Carousel": HOME / BOOKS & More

Under the search box, you will see **"a Carousel"** which has "HOME" in White letters.

*(If you look closely you will see a faint printing of BOOKS, VIDEO on right side of the word HOME.)*

This strip of words is called **"a Carousel"**.

You can touch **and hold finger down** on the word "HOME" and move finger to the "right" and the carousel will have the word **"RECENT"** where you can lift finger and tap on **"recent"** on carousel, and bring up pictures and icons **showing recent things** that you have pulled up on your Kindle.

Or if you put your finger back on the "carousel" **and hold finger down and drag to left** you will see more carousel subjects.

You will see **HOME / BOOKS / VIDEO / GAMES / SHOP / APPS / MUSIC / AUDIOBOOKS / NEWSTAND ...** listed on the carousel. Tap on the category that you want to appear on your screen.

If you tap on **BOOKS**, your book page will appear where you will see a partial list of the books you have purchased.

Also <u>under this list,</u> you will see a list of books "*<u>Recommended for you in Kindle Unlimited</u>*". Tap <u>on cover</u> of one of these books. <u>Information about that book will appear</u> on-screen:

You can get **<u>sample</u>** of the book *(free sample),* or you can **<u>purchase</u>** the book, or you can **<u>use the</u>**

**book** like a library book if you become a monthly subscriber to *"Kindle Unlimited"* ... go to Amazon for information about joining (for small monthly fee)  *"Kindle Unlimited"*.


**Return to Home Page** ... *(remember: tap that circle on bottom of screen to return home)*

## Library:  Apps That Are Downloaded

Beside the carousel listings, on right side of Home Page screen, you will see **a square symbol composed of 3 dots high and 3 dots wide ...** Under that symbol is the word **"Library"** ...

Tap on that symbol.

You will see **a listing of all your apps** *(opened apps and apps which you at one time downloaded and which may be reopened by clicking on the orange "arrow").*

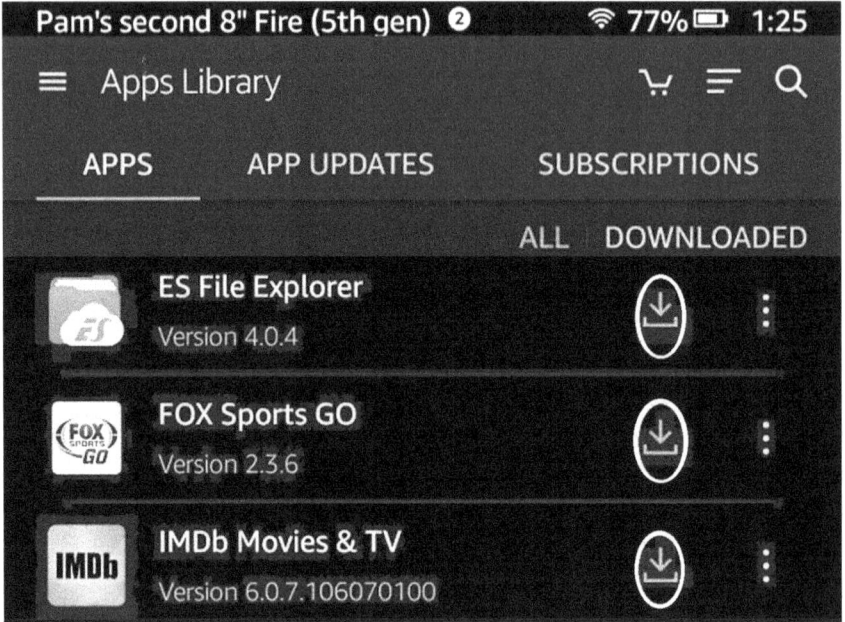

You will also see the words: **"ALL"** and **"DOWNLOADED"**

If **"All"** is in **gold color**, this means all apps are shown in the list of apps.

If **"Downloaded"** is in **gold color**, this means only those apps which you have downloaded to your Kindle are shown in the list.

Tap **"All"** if you want to see your entire list of apps.

Tap **"Downloaded"** if you want to see only downloaded apps.

If you want to open an app that is currently inactive, just tap on the gold "down arrow" beside that app and it will **"OPEN"** .

You will see the screen change beside that app listing. It will say "downloading" and it will show a line under the word downloading so you can see it is downloading.

When it is fully downloaded and OPENED, the colored line under "downloading" will go away and the word "downloading" will change to "OPEN".

## Icons On Home Screen: Highways

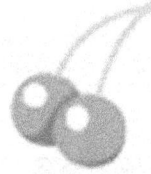

Under the carousel, **you will see several icons**.

These icons take you from HOME PAGE **directly**
- to **"Tune In"** radio,
- or to **"Silk"** *(which is the way to the Internet on*

*Kindle) / the Internet browser)* ,
- or to **Kindle books**,
- or to **Emails**,
- or to **Camera**,
- or to **Calendar,**
- or to **Amazon Music**
- or to **Amazon shop**,
- or to **Settings**,
- or to **Contacts**,
- or to **Photos**,
- or to **Weather** ... etc.

**Remember:** Start from **HOME PAGE** ... tap on **ICON** of where you want to go ... when finished, return to **HOME PAGE**, at least for now.

# 3. The Home Page: Everything Begins Here

## The Non-Computer Generations

The computer came into being in most households in the 1990's.

This means 6-generations of people living today are "non-computer generations". *(1930-1980's)* **We did not grow up with computers.**

The word Internet was unknown to most of us and when we first heard the word **"Internet"**, we said: **"What's the Internet?"** *(Never dreaming Internet would become such a major part of life.)*

**If you were born prior to 1990, you are the non-computer generation.** Amazing to think of it this way.

Many of you were forced into dealing with computers at some level because of your work, because of your job, so you began learning the fundamentals.

Others did not learn fundamentals and consider they cannot use e-readers and such. But they are not viewing this from proper concepts.

We, of the non-computer generation, have things to learn that younger generations take for granted for they don't even remember a time when there were no computers and no internet.

**Therefore, let's get started!** *(We can do it ... It is just a matter of instruction and practice.)*

## Highways

*__Home__ - to email/ to contacts / to shops / to radio stations /to PBS and other TV streaming/ to Kindle books /  to camera, taking photos, storing photos / to calendar /to weather / to maps / to clock / to apps / to Internet (and other things)*

From the **Home Page** you are going to begin your journey out from your house!  Almost everything begins from your "house" ... **from your Home Page on Kindle.**

**If we want to see "weather" we start at home, "Home Page", and <u>tap</u> on the "<u>Weather</u>" icon.**

We **tap** *(tap ... do not press or hold down ... just **tap**)* that icon and **instantly** we are at the **weather** where we can see weather information.

It is wonderful!

**Then when finished with the WEATHER**, we return **<u>HOME</u>**.

Tap the round button ***at bottom of Kindle screen***.

This is the highway back home. Home page will appear when you tap this round button. **<u>Tap</u>** ... do not press nor hold finger down.

# Home Is The Center Of Everything

**It is like your house is located in the middle and from your house you go directly to store. Then you return home and go directly to email and then you must return home before you go directly to another location.**

*There are <u>no side streets</u> taking you from email to camera.  <u>You must return home</u> from email and then go from home to camera, at least for now.*

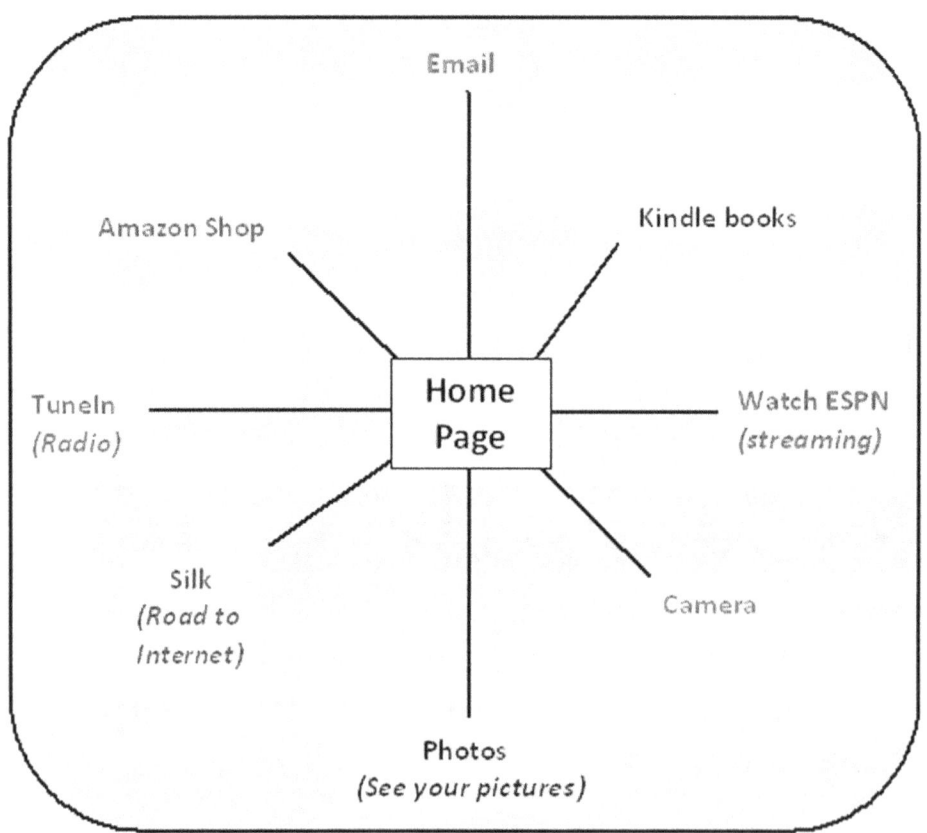

# Practicing:  Home Page To Each Icon

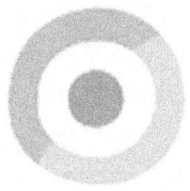

It is important to practice on your Kindle.  If you would take each of these chapters and practice everything, actually doing each thing on your Kindle device, it would pay big dividends and help ground you on the Kindle.

You may find it helpful to read a small section of a chapter (one instruction) and then take your Kindle and do that instruction on your Kindle.

Start with **Home page.**

Go to **first icon** on Home page.  *(tap on 1st icon)*

**Return** to Home Page. *(tap on circle at bottom of your screen to return home)*

----

From **Home Page** go to the **second icon** … tap on icon.

**Return** to Home Page.

----

From **Home Page** go to **third icon** … tap on icon.

**Return** to Home Page.

Continue from Home Page to next icon and back to Home Page.

Do this to each icon on Home Page screen.

By the time you finish, you should have a good understanding of highways from home to other places and back to home.

Practice this until you have concept in you and until it is automatic in your thinking.

Practice is very important in almost everything in this life.

## Your First Shopping Trip

**Now you decide you want to go shopping.**

Start your trip from the Home page. If you want to go shopping at **Amazon**, **tap** on **the Amazon "Shop" icon on your Home page.**

**Tap on .....**

The Amazon store will appear on screen. **Tap inside the search box** at the top of the screen and a keyboard will appear at the bottom of the screen:

**You can begin shopping** by typing the item in the Amazon search box and **tap** *(one time)* on **the yellow circle** at bottom of keyboard.

A list of merchandise will appear on screen. You may make your selection of item.

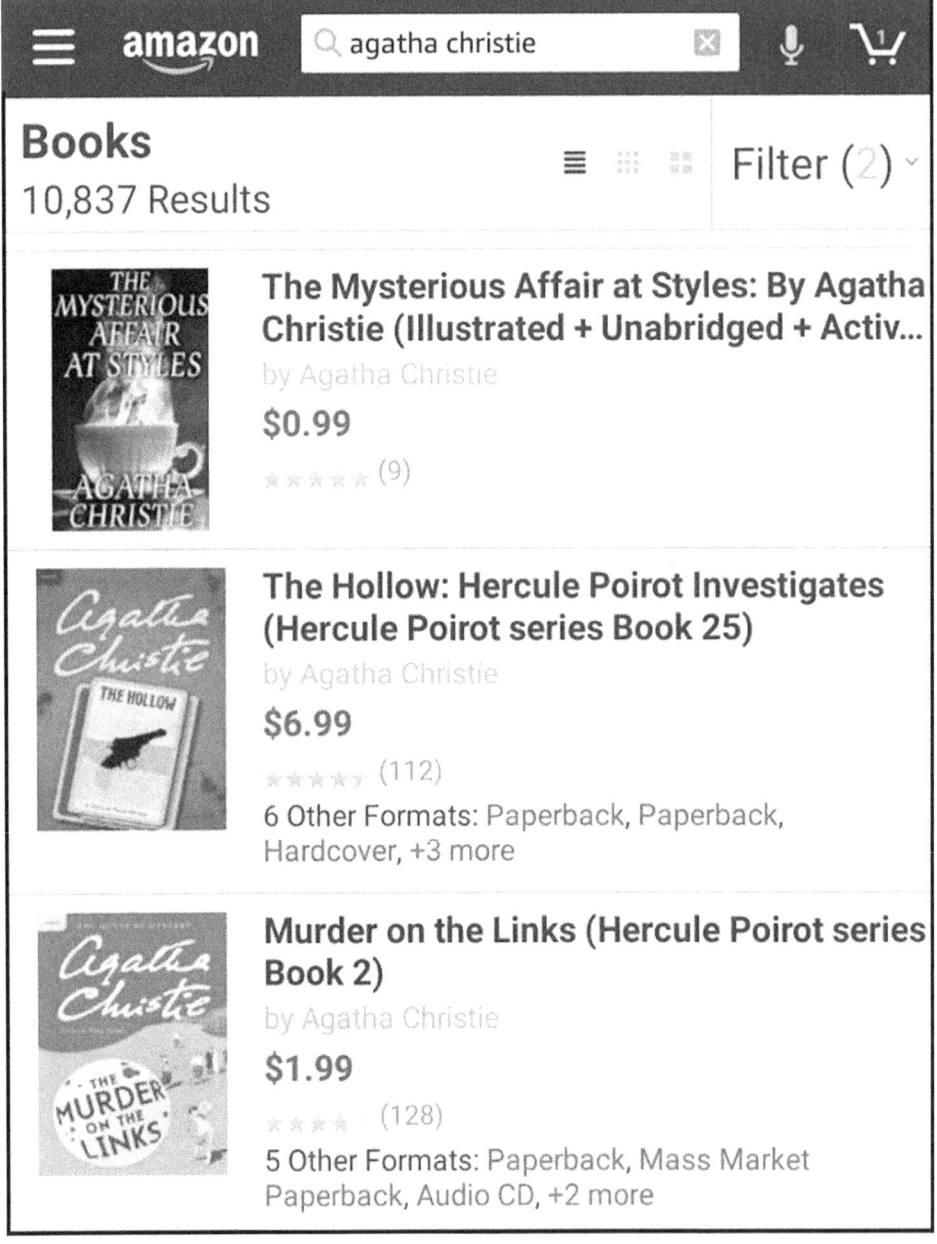

**Tap (one time) on the desired item in that list.**

**Another screen will appear showing cost of book and giving you an opportunity to order book.**

If you wish to purchase the item, **tap on the yellow rectangle** that has the word **"buy"**.

You can receive a FREE sample of the book by one tap on the "Download Sample"

The screen turns black as the book begins to download to your kindle.

Another screen will appear showing the BOOK and it will say "READ NOW" (yellow strip) **Tap on READ NOW and the book will open on the screen.**

Tap on the circle at the bottom of the screen to return HOME.

**(If there is no circle on bottom of screen, tap on bottom of screen and the circle should appear. You can also make the circle appear by swiping upward from the bottom of screen.)**

On the Home page tap on **BOOKS** in the carousel on your Kindle.  Your BOOK screen comes up.

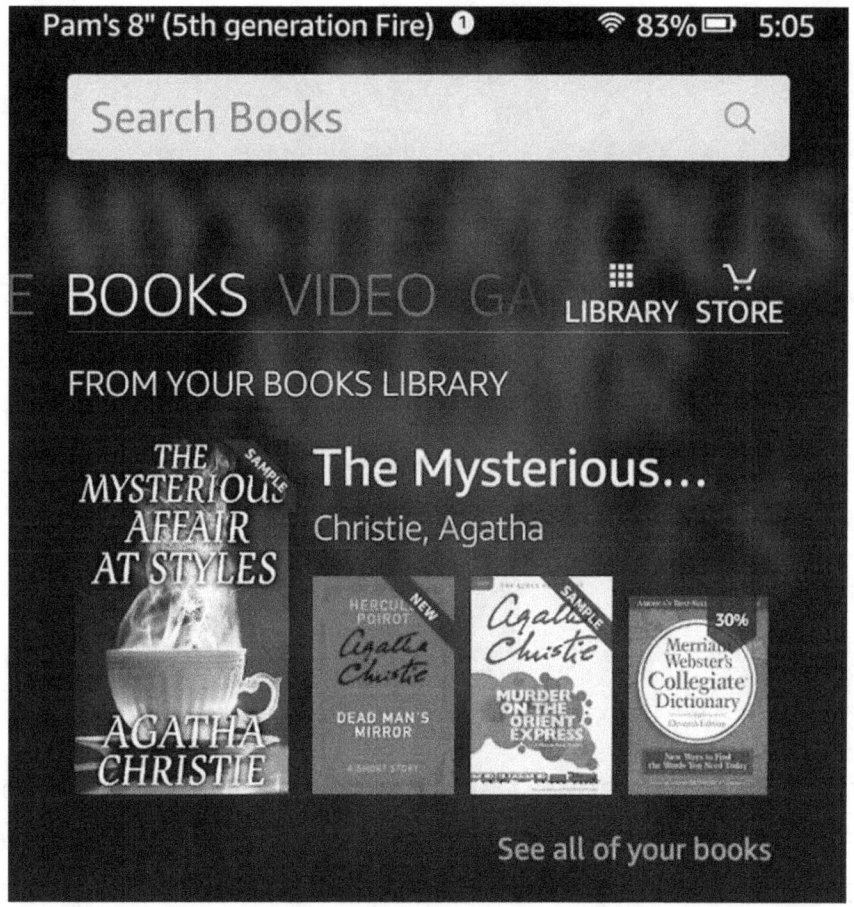

Tap on a book cover and begin reading the book.

So from Email, or Amazon, or from looking at the photos you have made, **you return home by one tap on the circle located at the bottom of the screen on the Kindle device.**

# Getting From Home To The Internet

You can go around the world on the **Silk** highway.

*(connection with the Internet / World Wide Web).*

At the Home page, tap on the **Silk icon**

Now you can access the Internet. You can type in the search box to locate items, information about people or events, radio stations, search engines such as Google or Bing. *(Tap yellow icon at bottom right side of keyboard to bring up selection made in search box.)*

You then return <u>HOME</u>  **(Home Page)** by **one tap** *(do not press or hold down finger, just tap)* **on the round button** at lower border of the screen on Kindle.

# All Highways Start At Your Home Page

All roads lead **in a straight line** ...

- **from your home** to the business **and back to home**

- **or from your home** to the TV show **and back to home**

- **or from your home** to the Radio station **and back to home**

- **or from your home** to the shopping store **and back to home**

-**or from your home** to the Email connection **and back to home**

Later you may discover some side roads, but for the time being assume you cannot go directly from Email to Shopping.  First you must return **HOME.** *(the* **Home Page)**

**Remember:**  The road leads **directly** to your HOME **when you tap the circle at the bottom of your screen.** *(Tap lightly ... do not press)*

# Everything Begins / Ends At Home Page

**If you are reading a book and you don't see <u>the round shaped button</u> on bottom of screen,  <u>tap on the screen</u>...** the "**round**" home button should then appear on bottom of screen.

**If you still don't see it**, **<u>tap again</u>** on the screen.

*<u>(Tap ...</u> do not hold finger down, nor press ... just <u>tap.)</u>*

<u>If this doesn't work,</u> **place your finger at bottom of screen and hold finger down and move finger toward top of screen ("swipe finger" or "drag" screen).**  You should then see the icon which allows you to return to Home Screen.

*(on the Kindle there is often more than one way to accomplish the same thing)*

**<u>So</u> you may be reading a book on your Kindle and decide you want to write and send an email.**

But you see no HOME page button.

**<u>Tap</u>** on screen *(just tap / don't press finger down)*

Now the **<u>HOME page button</u>** should appear.

**<u>Tap</u>** on that round button ... and **<u>HOME PAGE</u>** *(with all the icons/highways to other places)* appears.

From **Home Page** you can now tap on the **Email icon** and write your email.

**When finished with Email, <u>return home again</u> by one tap on the circle at bottom of Kindle screen.**

This takes you back home, and **<u>THE HOME PAGE</u>** appears again on your screen.

# 4. Settings: 1

There are multiple setting options on the Kindle and these make it easier for you, personally, to navigate about the Kindle.  It is like arranging your own desk at home.  You have preferences.  This chapter is about preferences and giving you options which suit you better.

## Brightness Of Screen

**Press your finger on top of Kindle screen** *(at the right side of the name of the device)* **and drag finger down toward center of screen.**

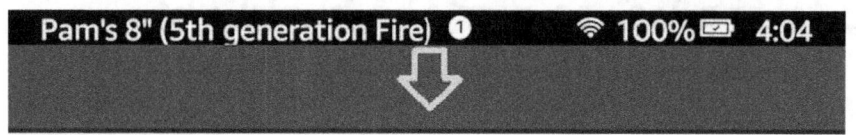

A menu will appear on top portion of screen.  This is a very easy way to get to the place where you can adjust brightness of screen and you can do this from each location on Kindle:  *(from a book, from a web-site ...)*

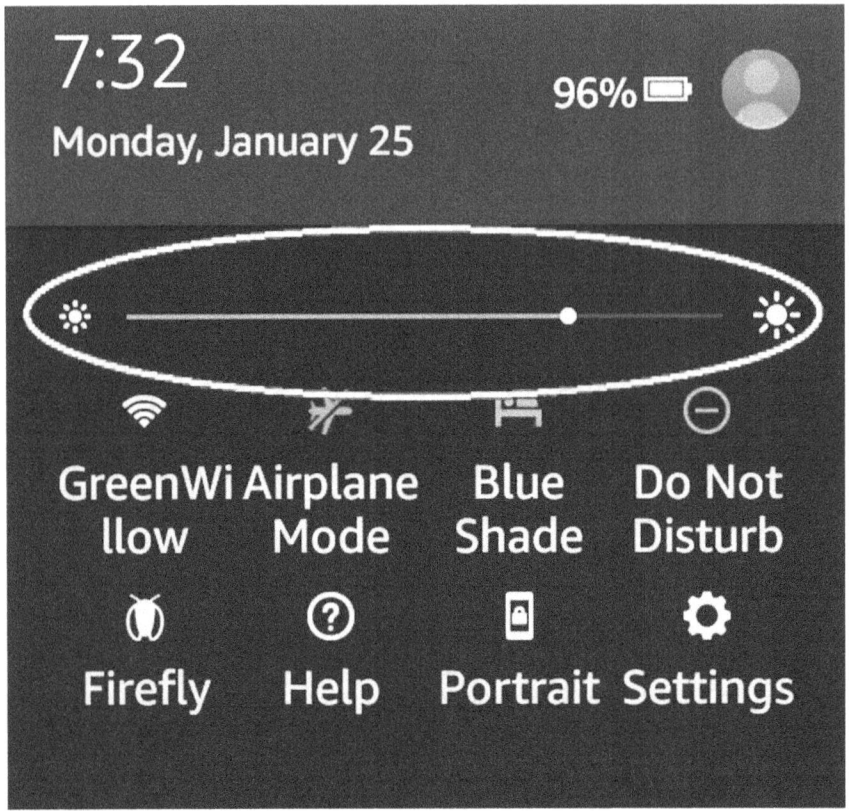

**Press finger on the white ball at the end of the yellow line and drag finger to the right to make the Kindle's backlight brighter.**

**Drag to the left to dim the backlight.**

Return to the Home screen with one tap on the circle at the bottom of the screen

# Adjusting Size Of Print

## Books:

**Bring a book on screen and tap in the center of the page.**

**A menu bar will appear at the top of the screen as follows:**

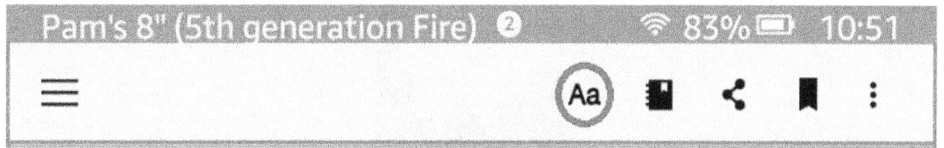

**Tap Aa.** The following will appear on screen:

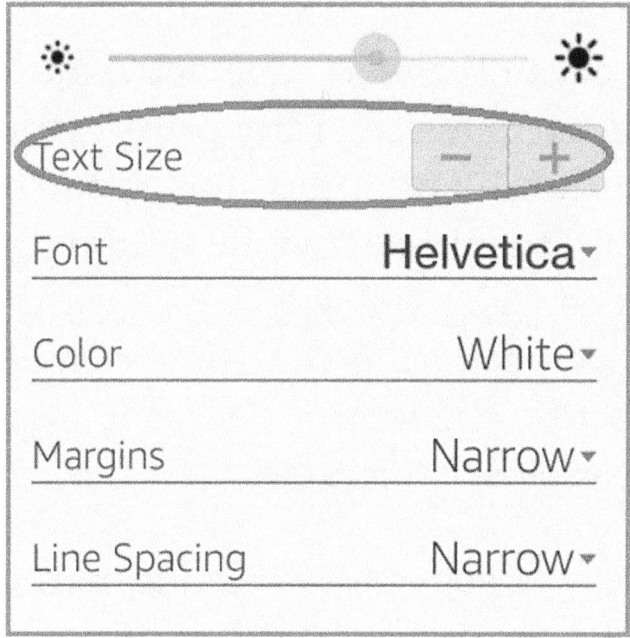

**Print size increases or decreases each time you tap on the plus or minus.**

**When you have the size to your preference, it will remain that way on your book settings.**

## Internet:

From **Home screen** tap **Silk Browser** icon ...

When you get to the web page you want to use, you can adjust the size of the print by putting two fingers (or thumb and index finger) on the screen, and dragging them apart while holding them down on the screen. You will see the size of the print enlarge as you separate your fingers and you will see the print on the screen decrease in size as you move fingers closer together.

This is a very effective and instant method of changing the print size on the screen.

**There is also an internal setting to change print size for the Silk Browser.**

At top of a web page, there are 3 horizontal lines one on top of the other, in upper left-hand corner of the screen.

Enter search term or URL

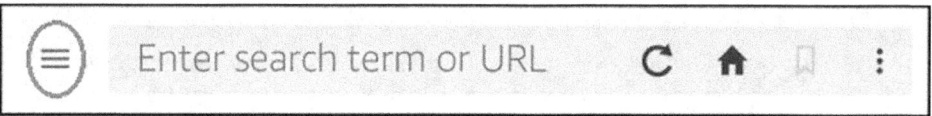

**Tap on: 3 horizontal lines**. The Amazon Silk menu displays ...

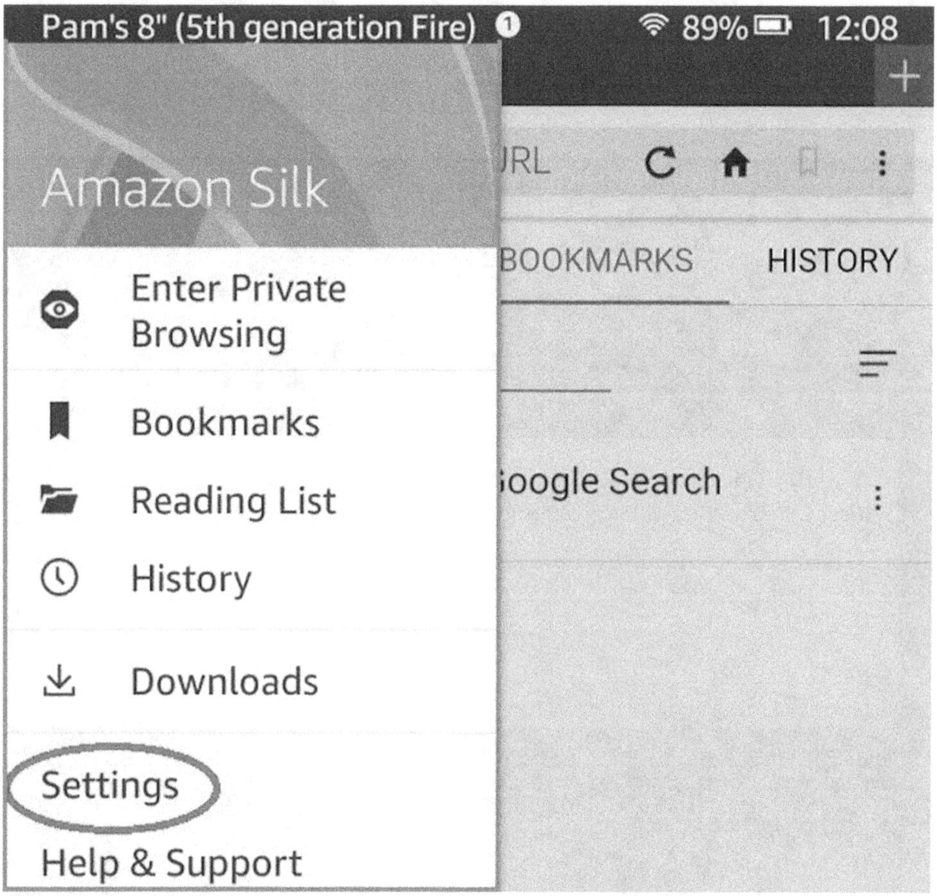

Pam's 8" (5th generation Fire)
89%
12:08
Amazon Silk
RL
BOOKMARKS
HISTORY
Enter Private Browsing
Bookmarks
Reading List
History
Downloads
Settings
Help & Support
oogle Search

## Tap on:  Settings

The following menu appears on screen ...

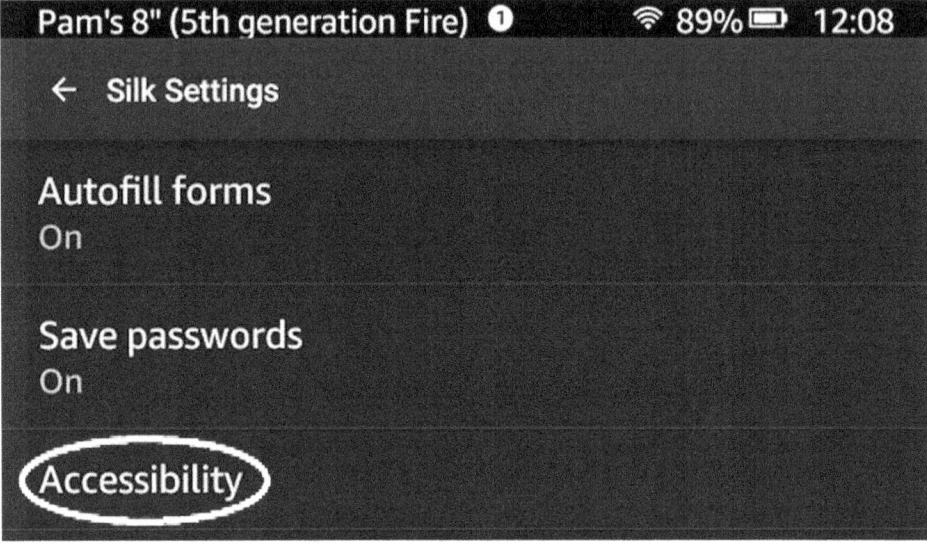

## Tap on:  Accessibility. The following appears ...

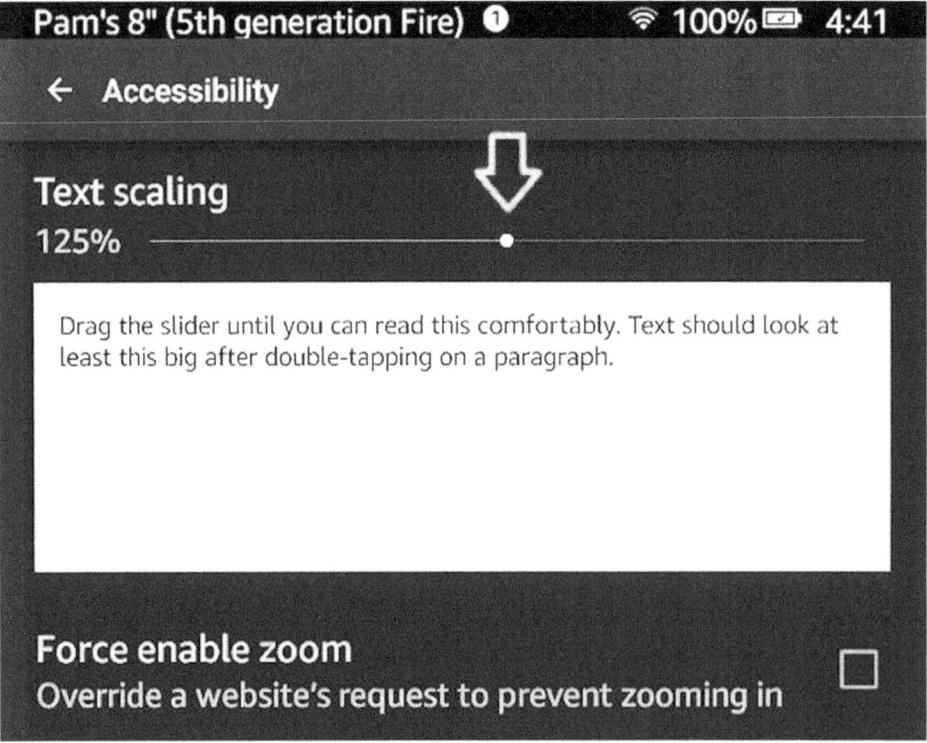

**Place finger on the white ball and move to right to make larger or left to make print smaller. You will see the size of the print in the text below the white ball.**

**The Internet print will remain the size you choose.**

**Notice on the screen: "Force enable zoom" (leave this unchecked) If the box has a check mark, tap and the check will go away.**

You can then **tap the triangle symbol** at the bottom of the screen.

This takes you to the Silk Settings screen.

**Tap the triangle symbol again**. This takes you back to the web page.

## Emails:

From the Home screen, tap on the Email icon:

On the Inbox screen, tap on the 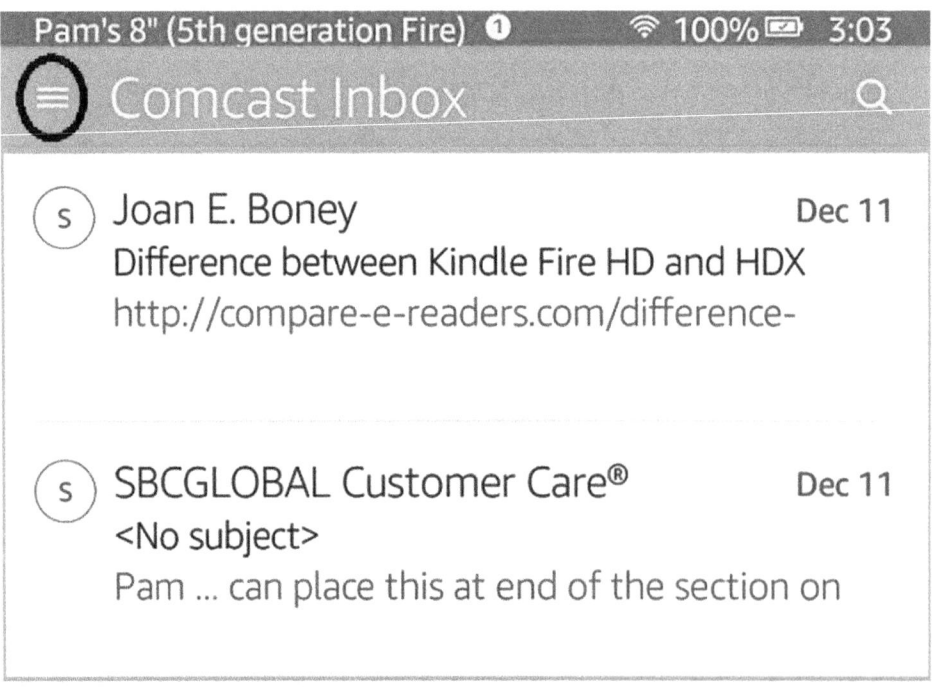 symbol in the top left corner of the screen ...

A narrow screen comes out from the left side of the screen ...

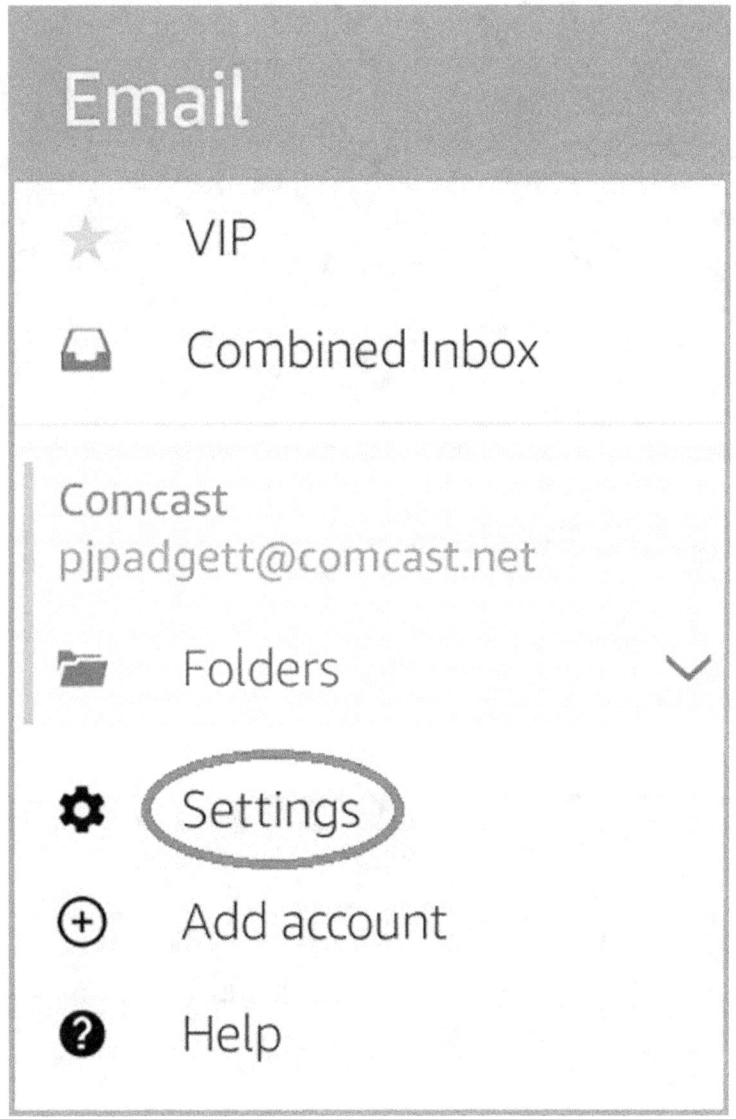

**Tap on Settings.**

Another screen comes up ...

**Tap on Email Settings.**

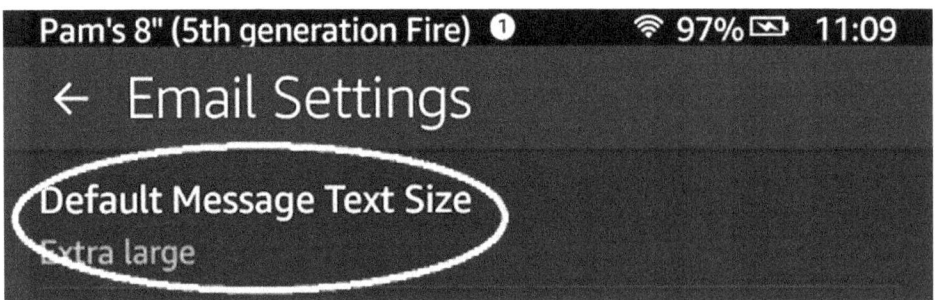

**Tap on Default Message Text Size**

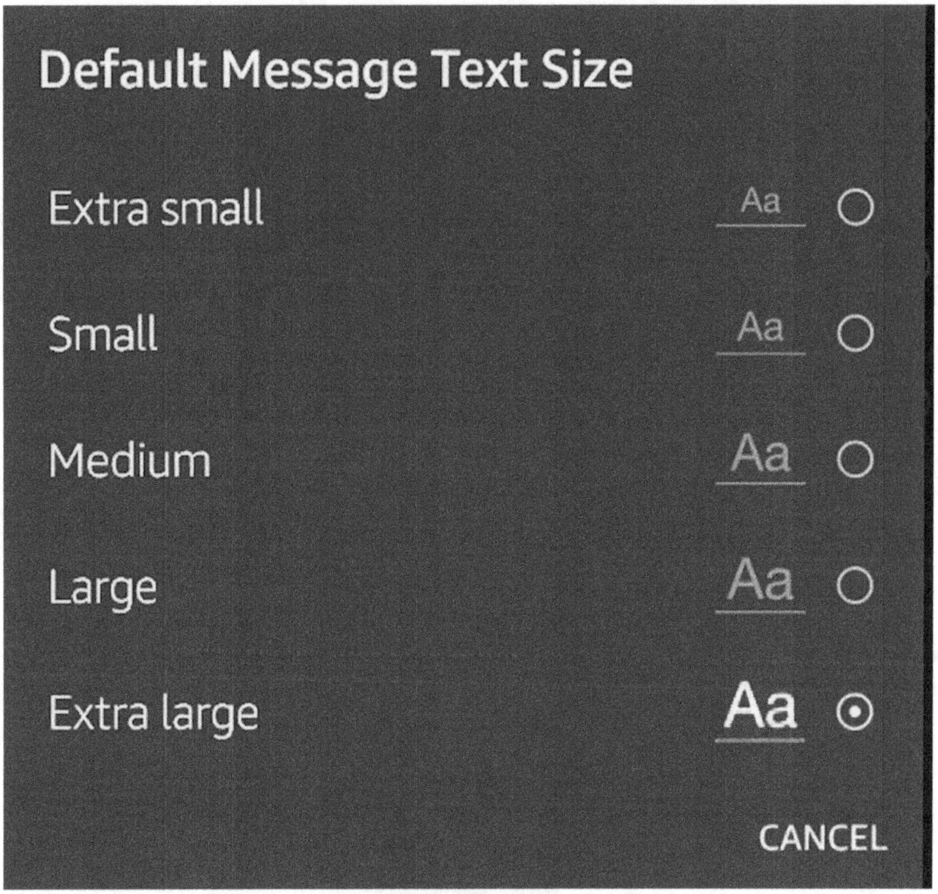

## Default Message Text Size

Extra small      Aa   ○

Small      Aa   ○

Medium      Aa   ○

Large      Aa   ○

Extra large      **Aa**   ⊙

CANCEL

**Tap on the size you want.** The previous screen (Email Settings) will automatically come up.

Tap the triangle symbol at the bottom of the screen, **twice**, to return to your Inbox.

After changing the print size, emails you open for the first time from your Inbox will use the print size you selected. Emails opened before you changed the print size don't show the new print size.

# Screen Rotation (Vertical / Horizontal)

You can use your Kindle in a vertical position or you can turn the Kindle to horizontal picture. You can also set Kindle to remain at vertical position or to remain at horizontal position.

**This is called "<u>Screen Rotation</u>"**

From the Home screen **tap on Settings** …

The Settings screen comes up …

**Tap on Display** and you'll see the Display screen:

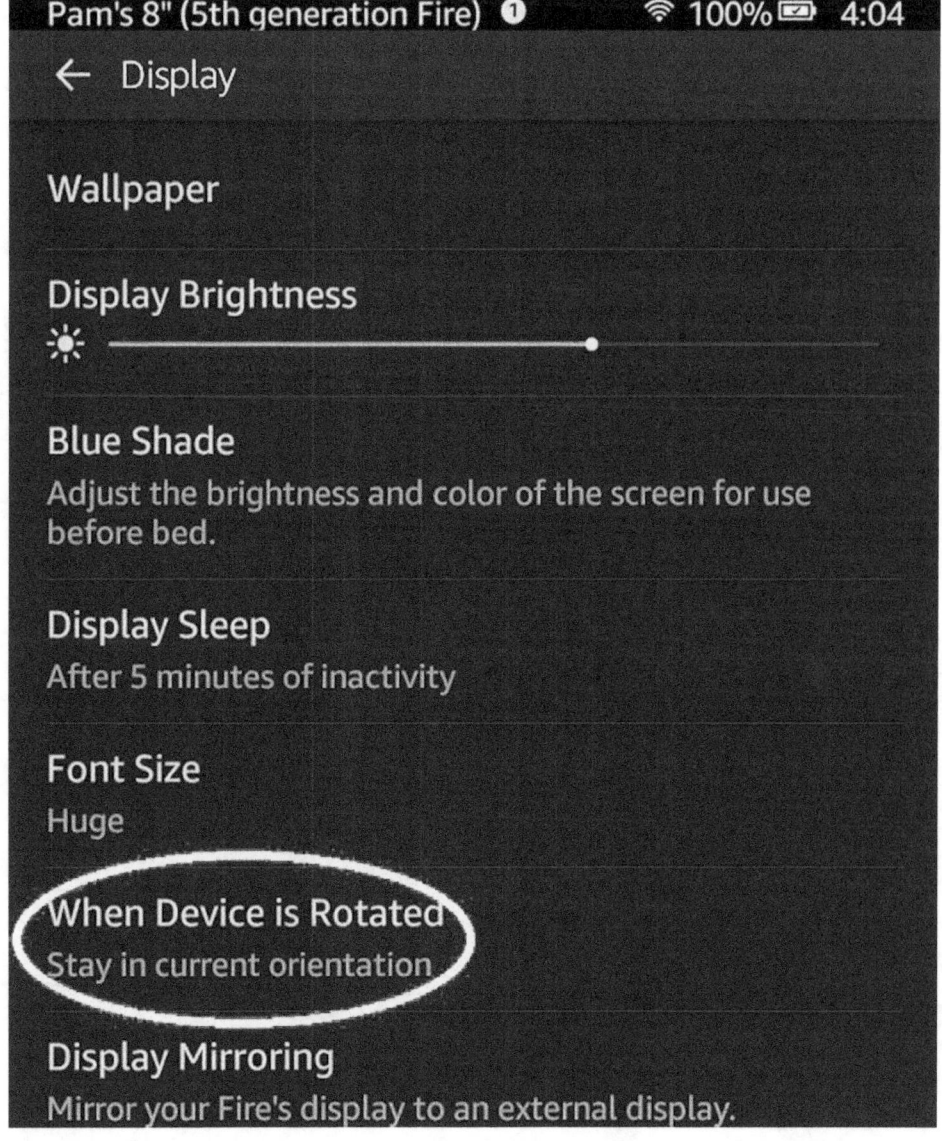

**Tap on:   When Device is Rotated**

A small screen comes up ...

## When Device is Rotated

○     Rotate the contents of the screen

◉     Stay in current orientation

CANCEL

Set according to your preference by one tap on the circle at the left side of the choices. The circle will light when you tap on your selection.

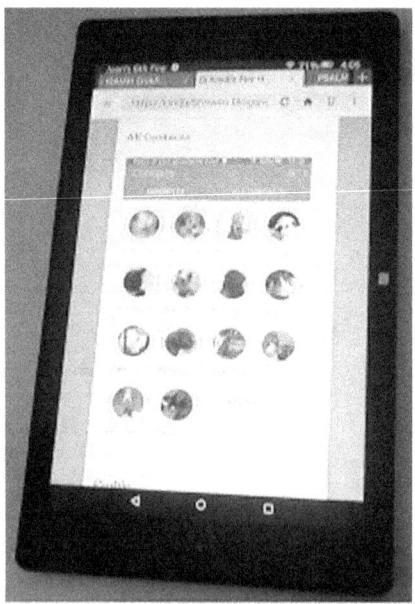

**Portrait**

For reading Books, the vertical *(Portrait)* setting is most used.

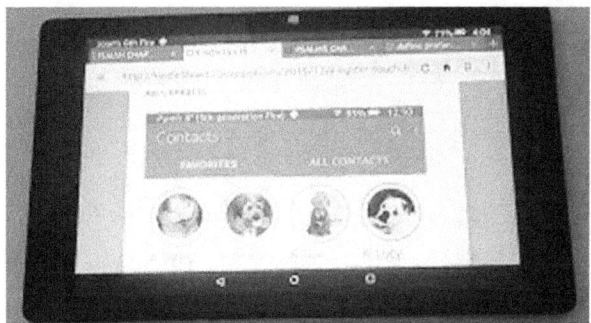

**Landscape**

For watching movies, TV, or to enlarge pictures on screen, the horizontal *(Landscape)* scene is usually preferable.

Return to the Home screen with one tap on the circle at the bottom of the screen ...

# 5. Settings: 2

## Notification Of Arriving Emails

The Kindle can be set to make a sound each time you receive a new email.

From the Home page, tap on "**Settings**"

The Settings screen comes up.

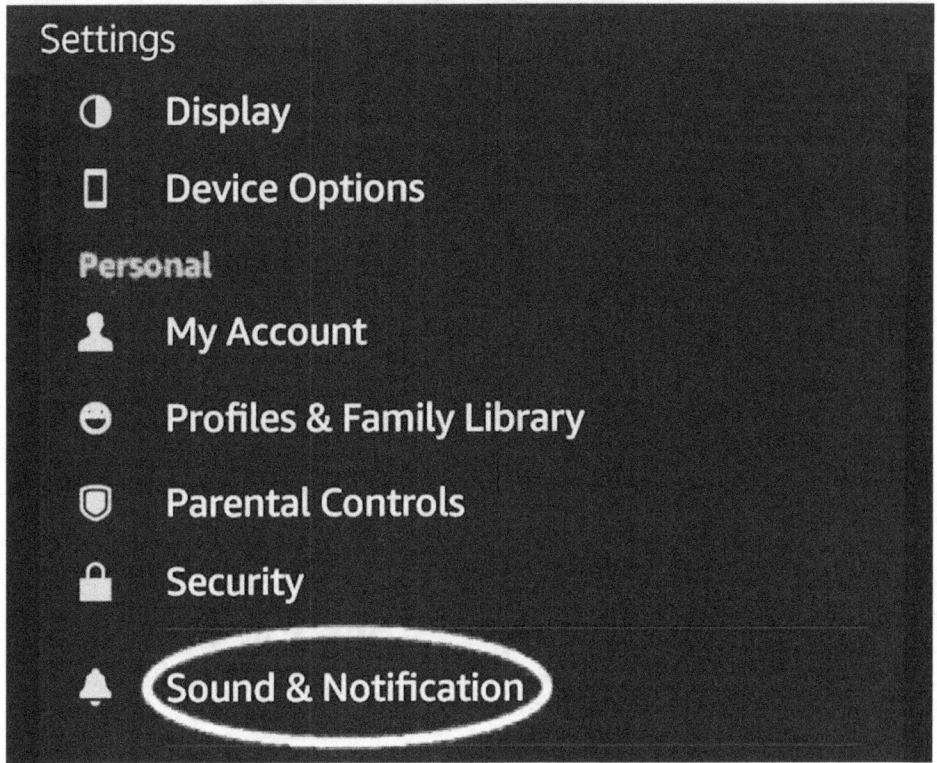

**Tap on "Sound & Notification".**

Another screen will appear.

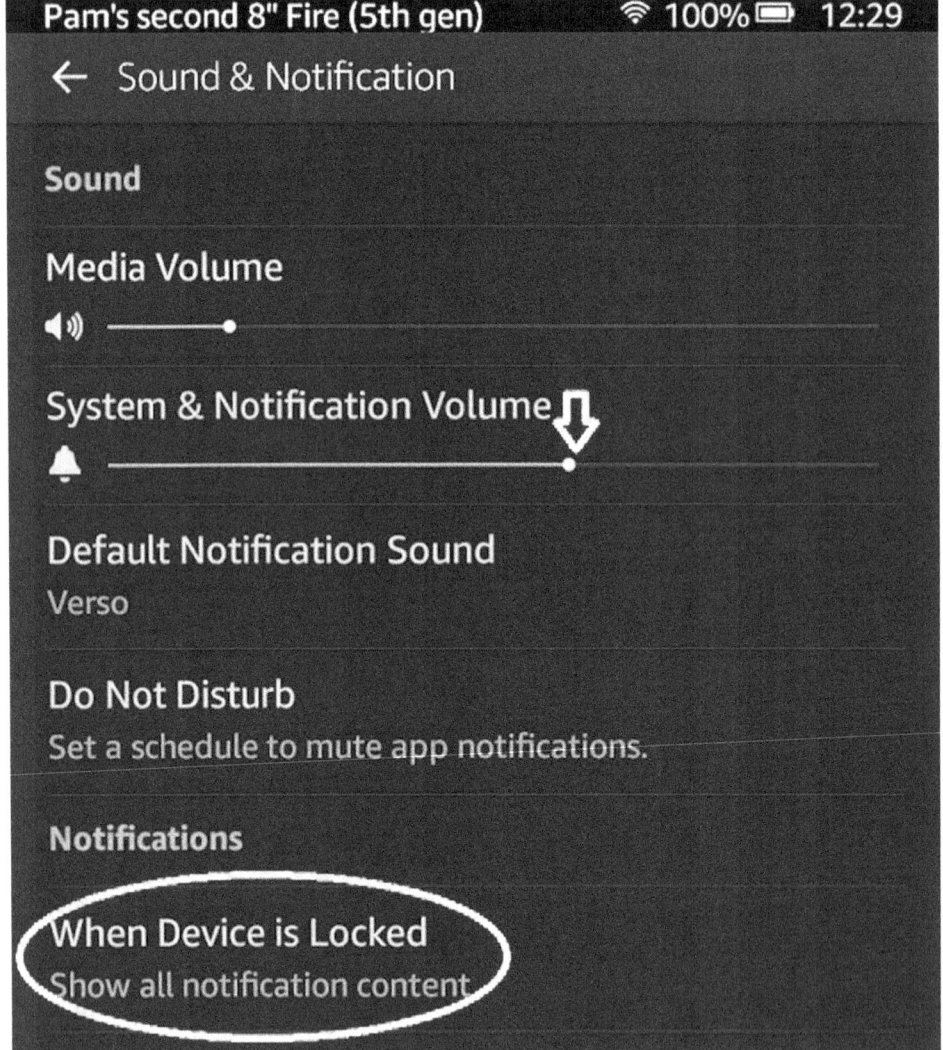

You can set the **volume** of the notification <u>by</u> <u>sliding the bar</u> which says:  "**System & Notification Volume**".

Tap on **<u>When device is locked</u>**.  A smaller screen comes on screen.

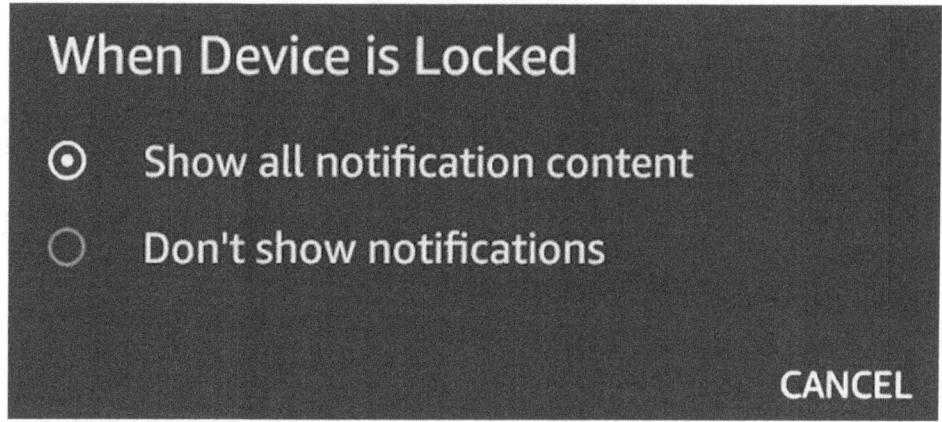

You can set the Kindle to notify you of arriving email.  Or you can set "Don't notify".

*(I have 2 Kindle units.  I set bedroom Kindle "Don't notify".  I would not want to be awakened by arriving emails in the middle of the night.  The office Kindle is set to "Notify" and a sound occurs each time email arrives on that Kindle.)*

Tap round circle at bottom of Kindle screen to return to the Home screen.

# Books: Fonts, Screen Color, Margins, Line Spacing

Tap on center of the page of a BOOK. A menu will appear at the top of the screen.

**Tap that symbol: Aa**

**The following menu appears on your screen, giving you the options of setting <u>font</u>, <u>screen color</u>, <u>margins</u>, <u>line spacing</u>.**

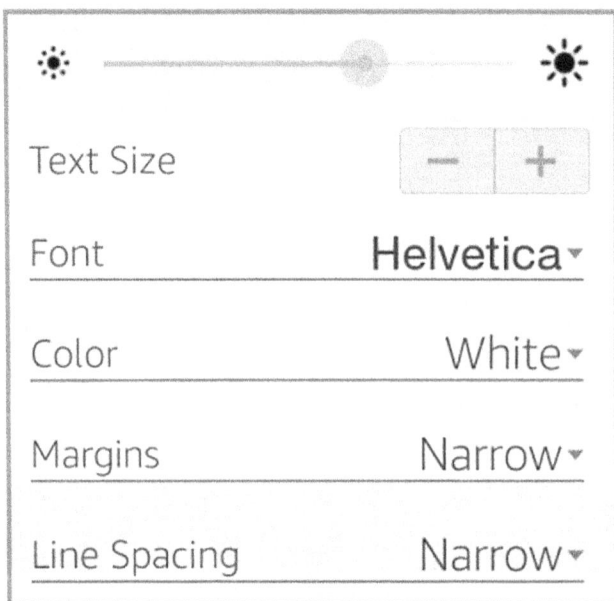

**Once you make these settings for one book, they should remain this way for other books so you do not have to change it again.**

**Font:**

When you tap on "font" the following choices appear giving you different appearances in the print.

| |
|---|
| Bookerly |
| Caecilia |
| Georgia |
| Palatino |
| Baskerville |
| Helvetica |
| Helvetica Light |
| Lucida |

**Tap on the names** until you find the style of print you like.

## Color:

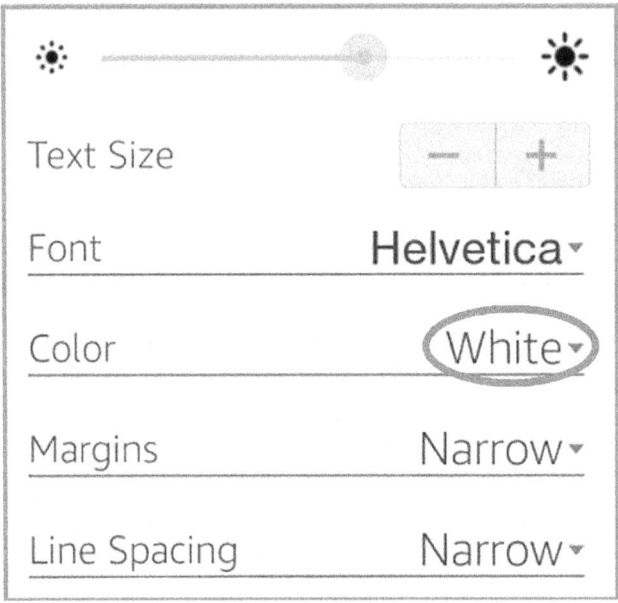

**Tap on white** and a screen appears giving you 4 choices of background: *white, black, sepia, green.*

**Tap on the color you want**.

For example, if you tap on "black", the page turns black with white print. *("Black" is very good for night reading in bedroom.)*

## **Margins:**

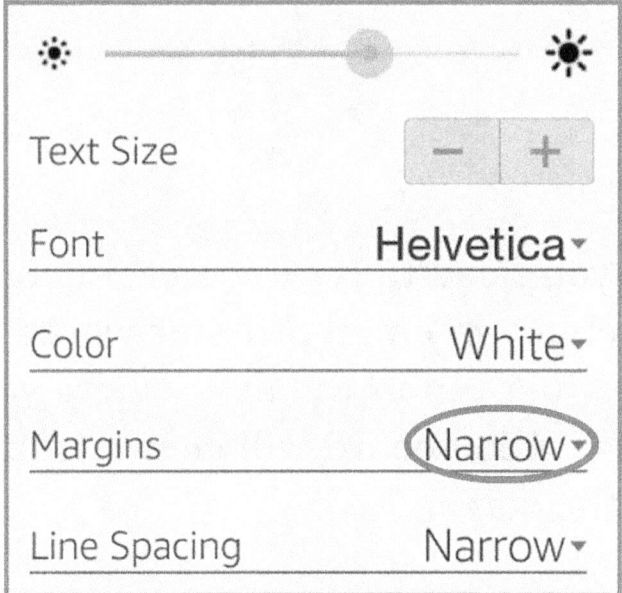

Three choices:  narrow, normal, wide  ... **tap on choice** ...

## **Line Spacing:**

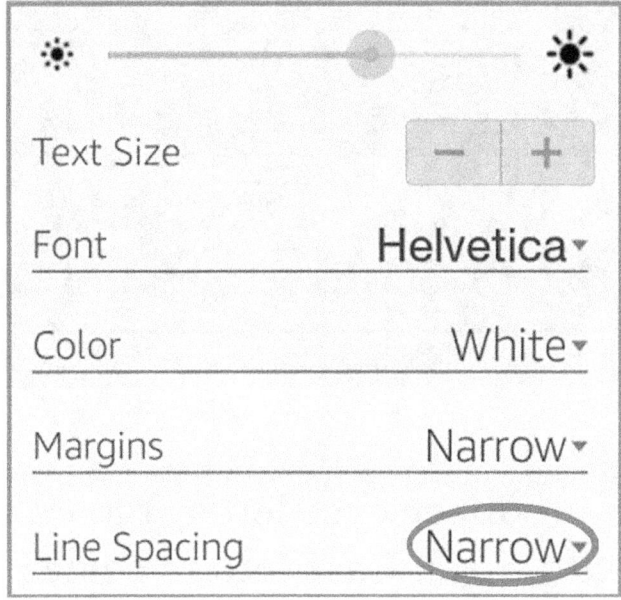

**Tap on choice:  narrow, normal, wide ...**

# Keyboards

Whenever you need to type something on your Kindle, such as an email or enter words in a search box, just tap in the area where you want to start typing. A keyboard will come up at the bottom of the screen.

The keyboard that comes up at the bottom of the screen may have only lower-case letters on it ...

If you need an upper-case letter, tap on  and a keyboard with upper-case letters comes up ...

Tap on 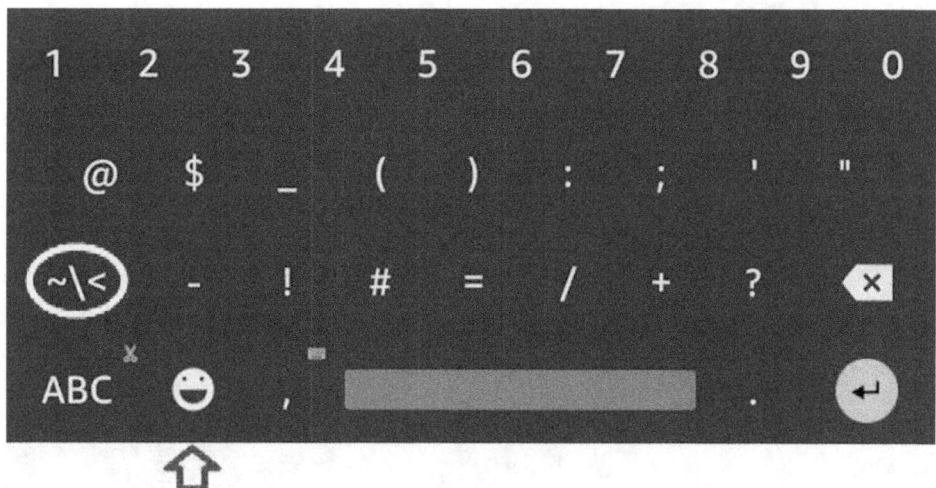 and a keyboard with numbers and punctuation symbols comes up ...

Tap on the smiley face  and special drawings (called emoji's) come up such as:

Tap on **~\<** and a keyboard with special characters comes up ...

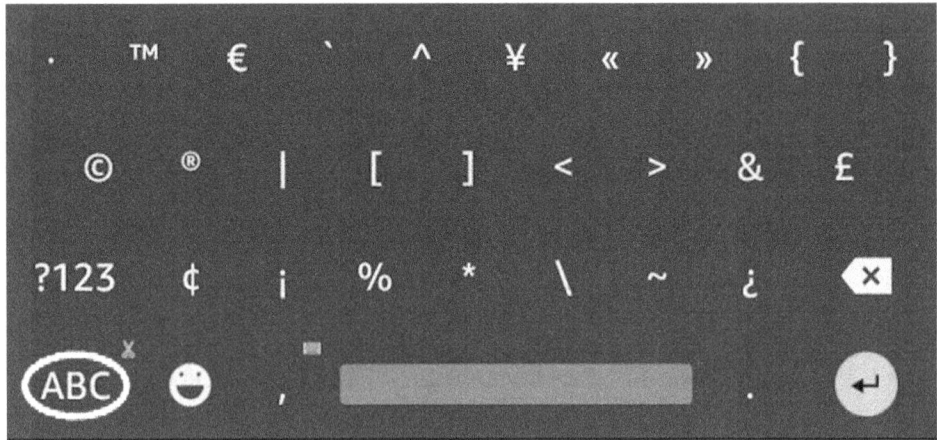

Tap on **ABC** and the basic keyboard with letters comes up again.

**There are two important keys on each of these keyboards, the Backspace key and Enter key.**

## Backspace key:

The Backspace key is used to delete letters you want to remove from something you have typed. Tap on the right side of the letter(s) you want to delete. Then tap on the Backspace key one time for each letter you want to delete. The letters will be removed.

## Enter key:

The Enter key can be used when you finish typing in a "Search" box. Tap on the Enter key and the search will start.

The Enter key may also be used when you want to start a new line or paragraph of typing, such as when you are typing an email. Tap the Enter key and the cursor will go to the next line. You can resume typing there.

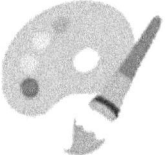

# 6. Moving Icons / Setting Wallpaper

On your Home screen there are several icons (*symbols*).

You can move the icons around so you can easily find what you want.

<u>For example</u>, icons used most often could be put on the first line.

## To Move An Icon

**Press <u>and hold</u>** your finger down on the icon you want to move.

**DRAG your finger, <u>without lifting</u>**, to the place where you want the icon to be on screen, <u>but not directly on top of an existing icon</u>... **beside** one.

After making sure the icon is not on top of another icon ... **then** lift your finger. The icon will stay there.

## Creating A File Of Icons

**Hold finger down on an icon** and after the icon "lights up" drag the icon **and place directly "on top" of the other icon that you want in the same file.**

<u>Release finger</u> and there will be a "file" where both icons are together on the icon part of the home screen.

The size of the icons in the file will be reduced in size and you will see the smaller icons side by side in the same location and under the file you will see "Folder 1" or "Folder 2".

You can get to the icon by **one tap on the folder** and then **one tap on the icon** you want to see which is inside the folder.

When finished with the icon **you can return to home screen** by one tap on that circle at bottom of page **and then by a second tap** on the circle at bottom of page.

**To change the name of the folder**: Tap on the icon of folder that is to be renamed.

A screen will appear saying "Folder ___" and both icons that are in the folder will appear in the box under the name of the folder.

**Tap on the name of the folder.** A keyboard will appear on bottom of the screen.

A blinking vertical line will appear in the area where the FOLDER NAME is located ... **tap at the end of the folder name and the blinking vertical line will place itself at the end of the folder name** ...

Then you can use the backspace key

located on the keyboard and remove the name of the folder **by backspacing through the name**.

Type the new name into the space ...

Tap the home key (round button at bottom of screen).

The new name will appear in the icon group on your Home Page.

## Warning About Removing Icons

Kindle arrives with many pre-installed icons on your home page. Other icons will appear on your Home Page when you order various apps such as PBS streaming, CBS/ABC/NBC/ streaming.

It may seem cluttered to you and you might think you want to remove **"unnecessary"** icons.

In working with a woman to try to help her with Amazon Music, she could not find the icon which allowed her to get to Amazon Music. **Then she said when she bought her Kindle she removed**

**several of the pre-installed icons.** Also she had removed the PHOTO icon so she could not get to the picture she had taken. She became a member of Amazon Prime after removing the icons she felt **unneeded**.

**Now she needed those icons <u>but they were gone</u>!**

**She went back to original settings to get everything back. This meant she had to go through the basic installation again on her Kindle.** *(When you do this, you might end up losing some of your content and have to place such things as "email contacts" back again on your Kindle.)*

**<u>Instead of removing icons</u>** which you consider unneeded from your home screen, **it would be better to group those icons into a folder of 4 icons.** This makes the icons smaller so they aren't as cluttered looking and yet you still have them on your home screen if you need them later.

# Wallpaper (Screen Background)

From the Home screen **tap on Settings** ...

The Settings screen comes up ...

**Tap on Display.** The Display screen comes up.

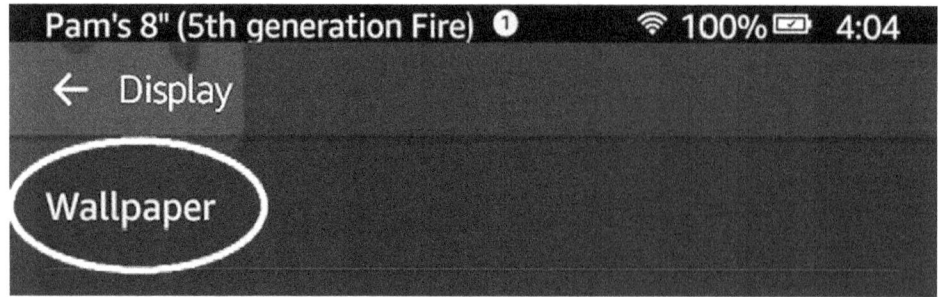

**Tap on Wallpaper**

A screen appears showing the current wallpaper.

At the bottom of the screen are other wallpaper options available. **Tap on the wallpaper option**

**you want to use.**

The selected wallpaper will now display on the screen. Two buttons also display ...

**Tap on SET**

Return to the Home screen with one tap on the circle at the bottom of the screen ...

# 7. Email Contacts: Create A Contact

**Set up your own name on your contact list.** That way you can practice sending emails by sending email to yourself. Also when you use the microphone for dictation, you can dictate email to yourself.

There are two ways to set up a contact.

You can set up a contact from an email.

Or if the only thing you have is an email **address** *(but no email),* then you will have to set up the contact manually.

**First we will explain setting up a contact from an email ...**

## From An Address Inside An Email

From your **Home page** tap on the Email icon:

Make sure you are on your **Inbox screen** by looking at the left side of the blue band at top of the screen.  The word "Inbox" should be there. ...

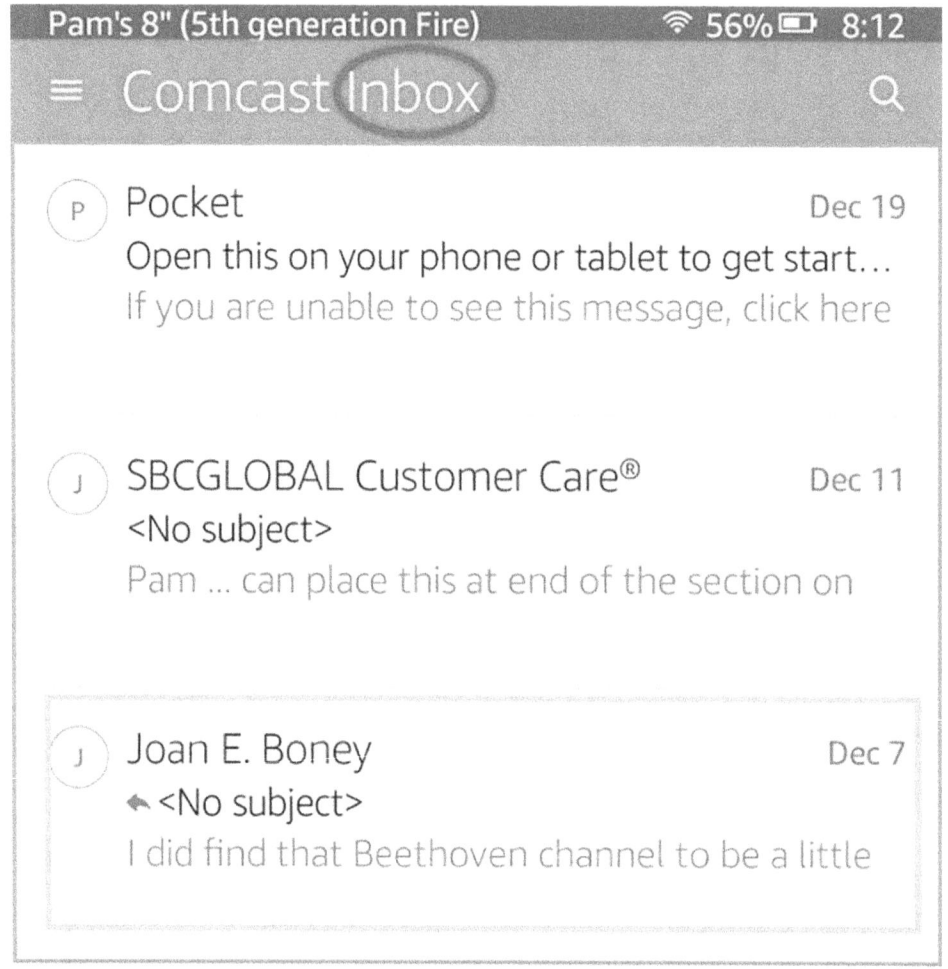

(*If you are on another email screen, on the left side of the blue band there will be an arrow pointing left.*

**_Tap on that arrow until you return to your Inbox Screen._**)

# Tap on an email with the person you want to add to your contact list.

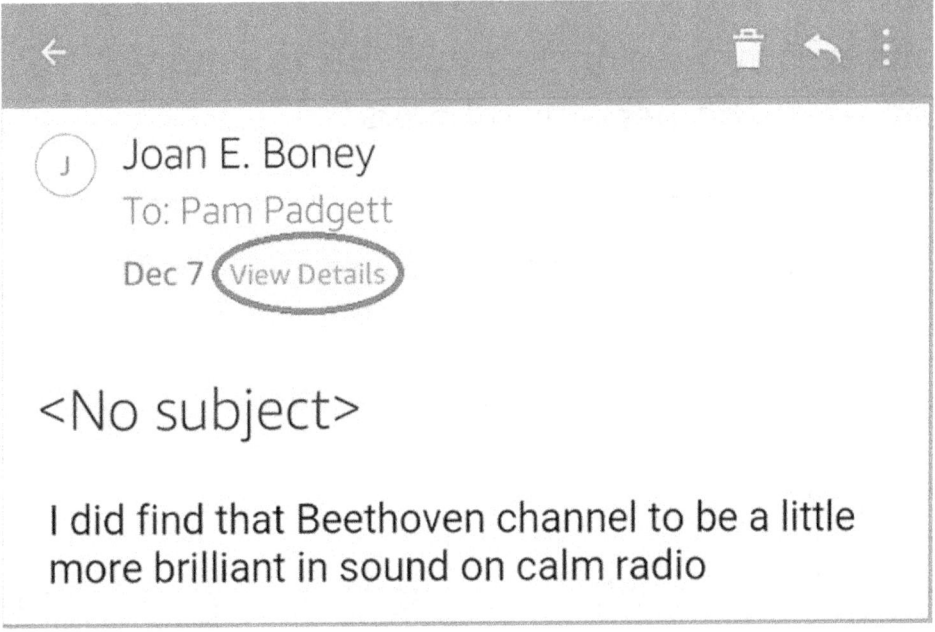

We need to see the email addresses. If the email addresses are not visible, **tap on "View Details"** near the top of the screen. The email addresses for the sender of the email and each person the email was sent to will be shown ....

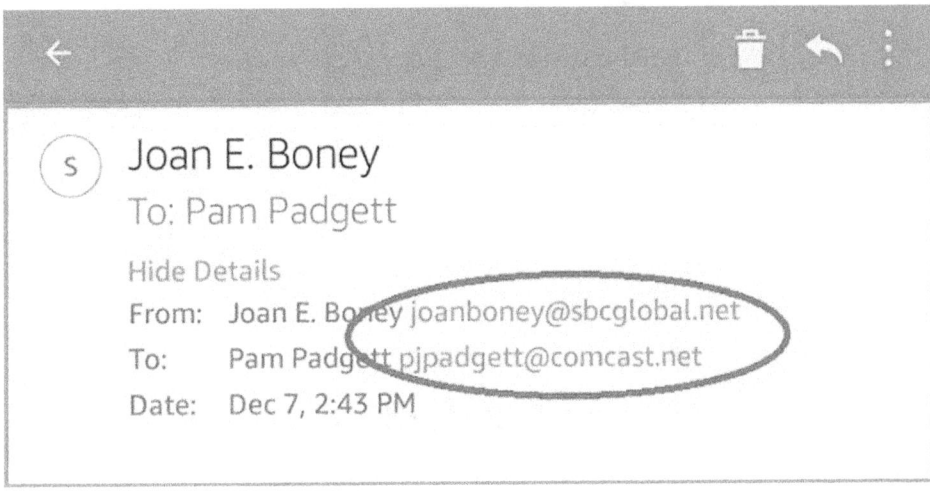

Tap on the email address of the person you want to add to your contact list.

A box will appear on screen with the email address of the person to be added.

**Tap on OK.**

Another screen will appear **with an orange band** at top of page. **Under that orange band,** you will see in the white background these words: **Create New Contact".**

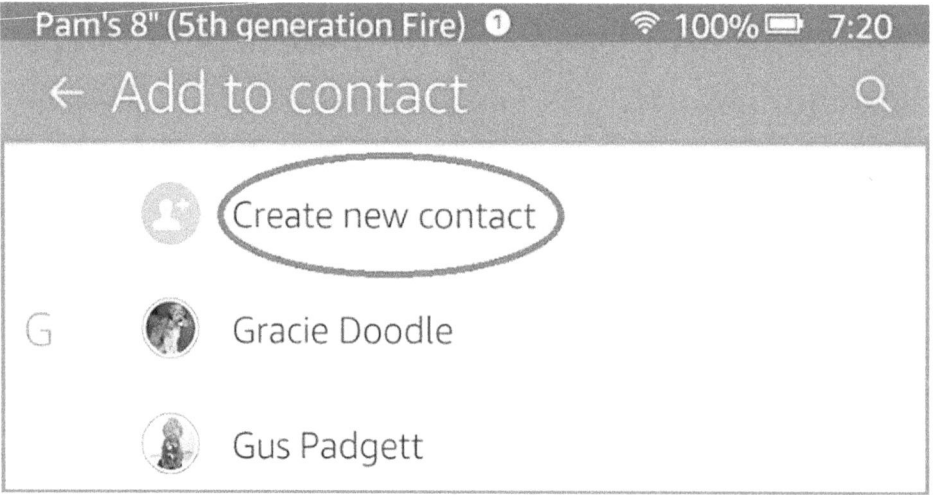

**Tap on "Create New Contact"**

Another screen appears with the person's name and email address filled in.  You can add additional information if you choose to do so ...

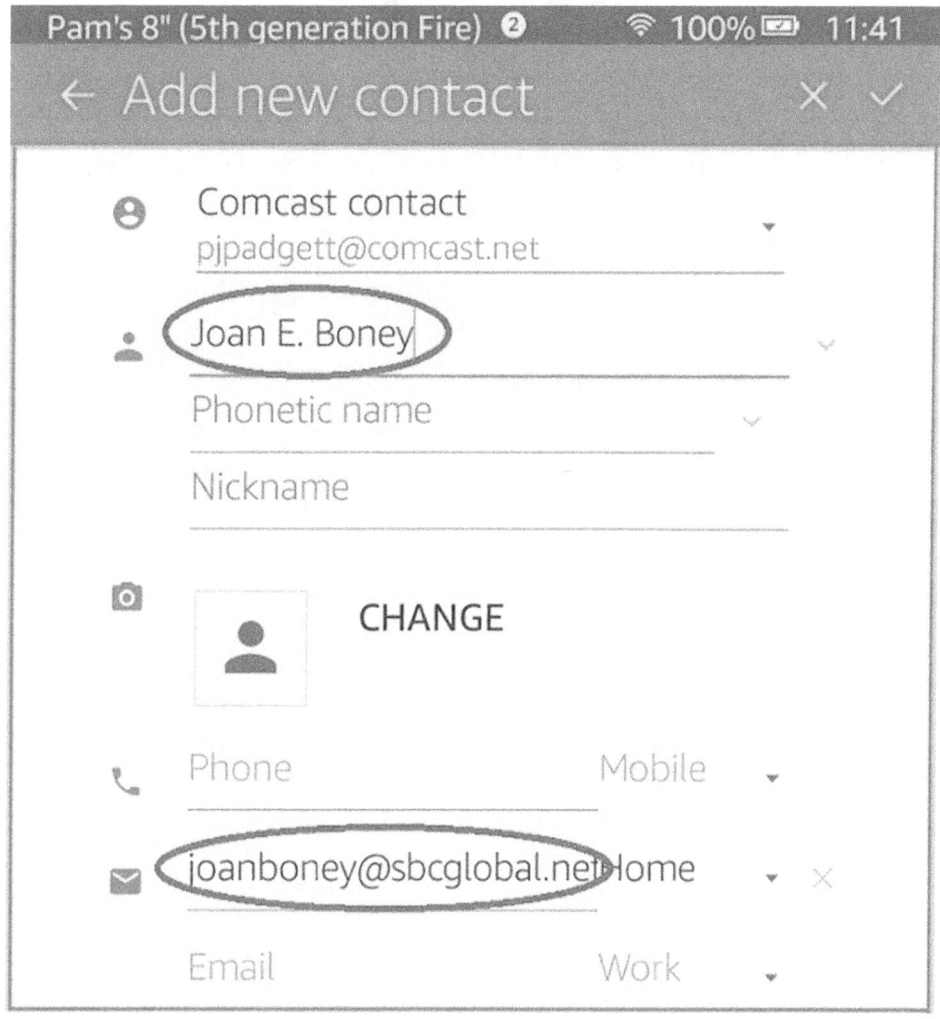

**Tap on Check mark** in upper right corner of screen.  (a notice will appear on screen saying "contact saved")

**To see your contacts, go to the Home page and tap on the Contacts icon.**

A
B
C
Contacts

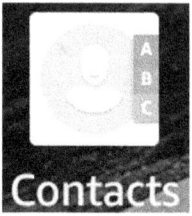

The new contact is listed on the Contacts screen.

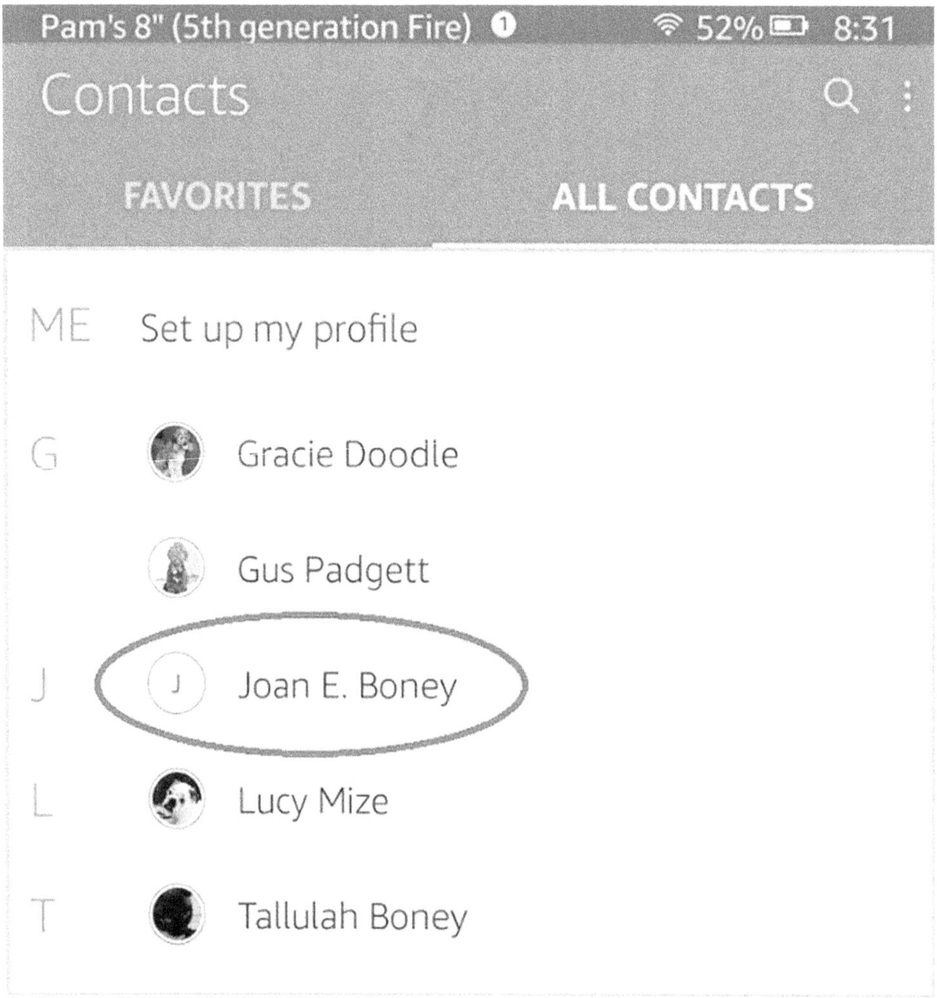
Pam's 8" (5th generation Fire)
52%
8:31
Contacts
FAVORITES
ALL CONTACTS
ME
Set up my profile
G
Gracie Doodle
Gus Padgett
J
Joan E. Boney
L
Lucy Mize
T
Tallulah Boney

## Manually:  From Email Address (With No Email)

### From Home Page ... tap on "Contacts" icon

You will need to be on the screen that says Contacts at the top.

*(If another screen comes up, tap the "back" arrow at the bottom of the screen*

*...until you get to the screen that says **Contacts** at the top)*

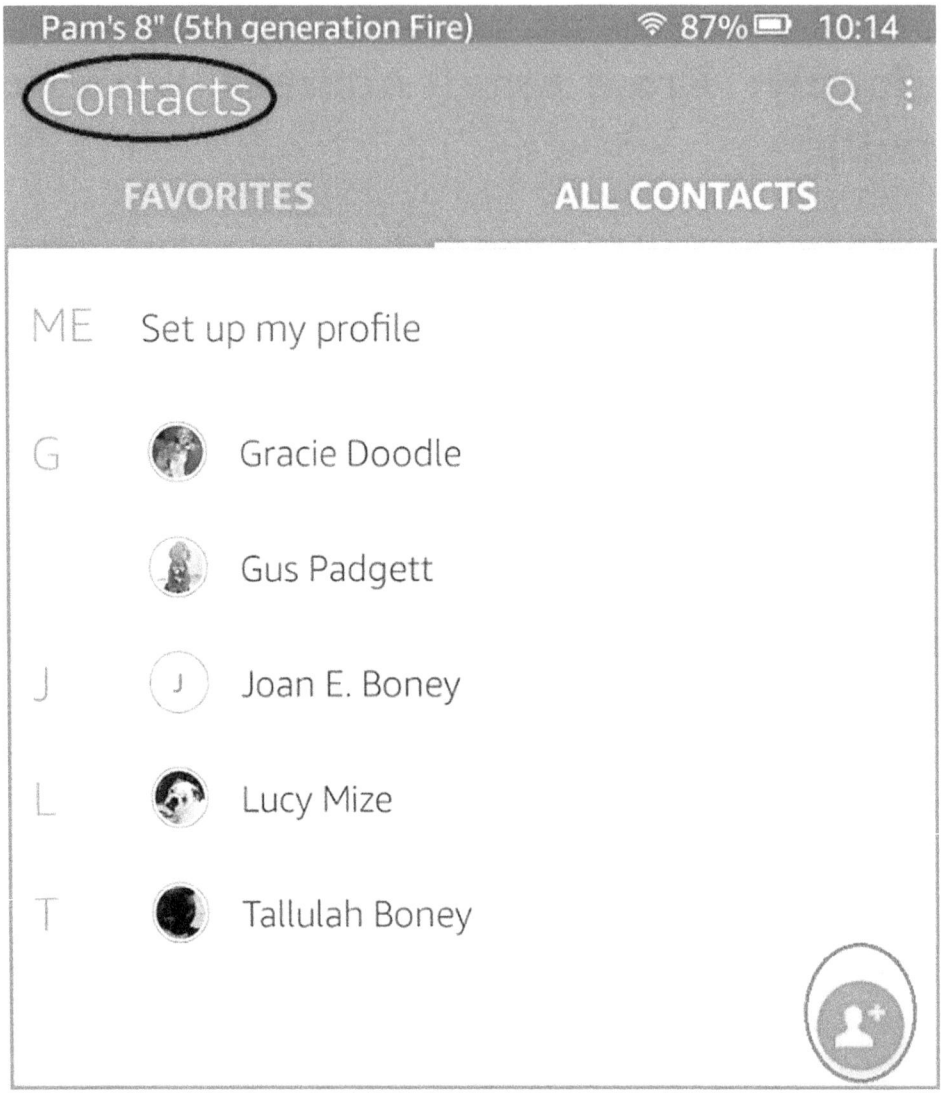

At the bottom right corner of the page you will see an orange circle with a silhouette and + sign.

**<u>Tap on this orange circle.</u>**

**The following profile page will appear on screen, with a keyboard on the bottom.**

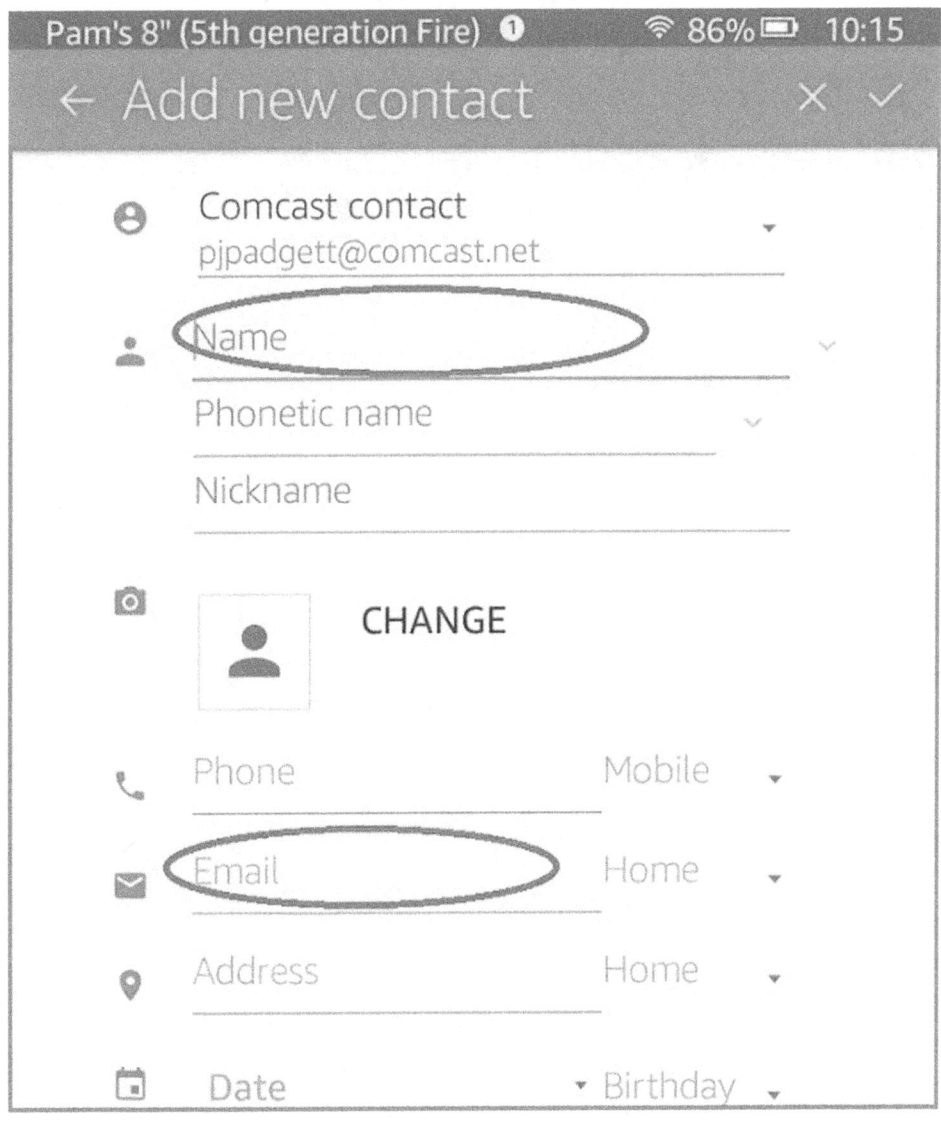

**Fill in name, email address and anything else pertinent.**

After you finish this profile page, **tap the check mark at top right corner of the screen.**

Another screen appears with name of person, phone number, email and such. *(showing that person has been added to your contact list)*

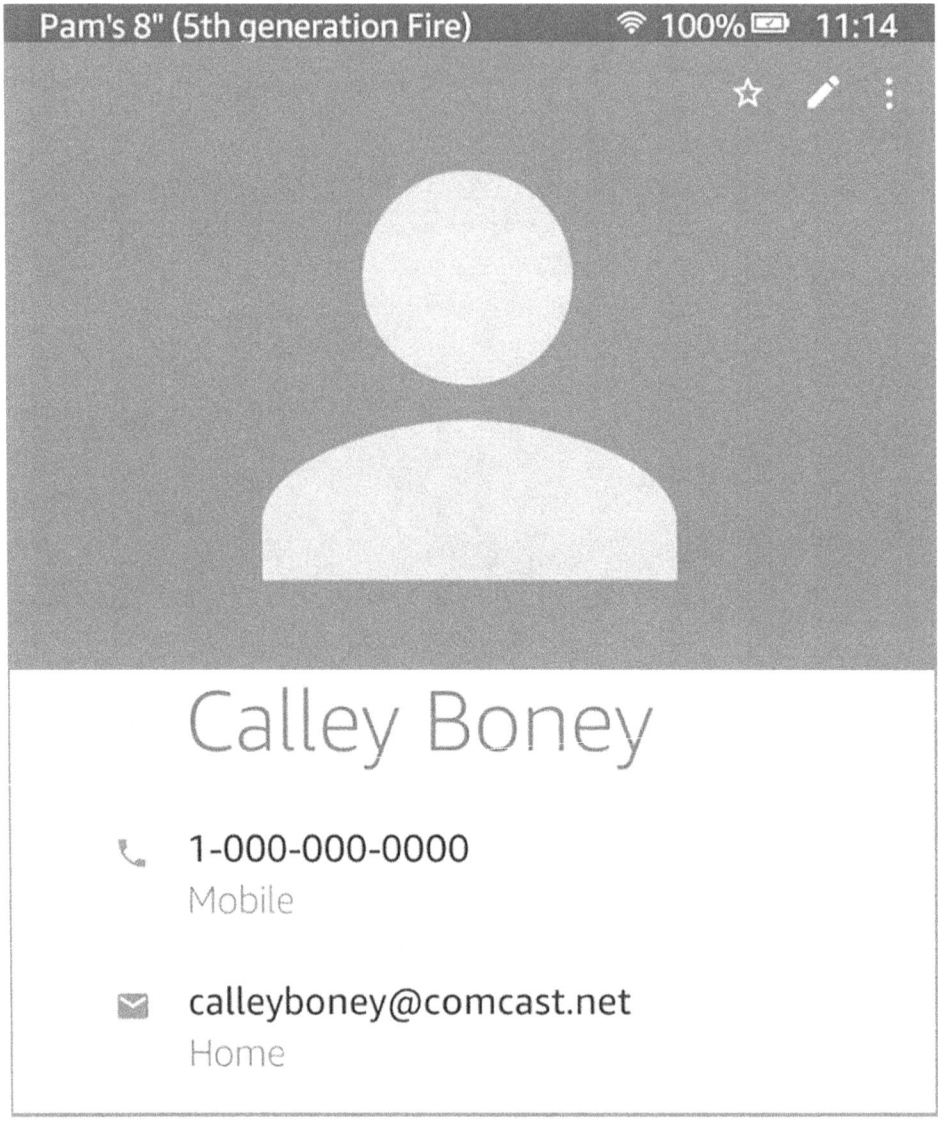

**(Remember:** Put your own name and email address on your contact list so you can use your email address to practice.)

# 8. Email Contacts: Editing / Settings Favorites

## Edit A Contact

You can edit (add or change) information for a contact you have already setup on your Kindle.

From the Home screen, **tap on the Contacts icon:**

*(You should see a screen with an orange band at the top of the screen with the word "Contacts" on the left side. If another screen comes up, tap the "back" arrow at the bottom of the screen*

*until you get to the screen that says Contacts at the top)*

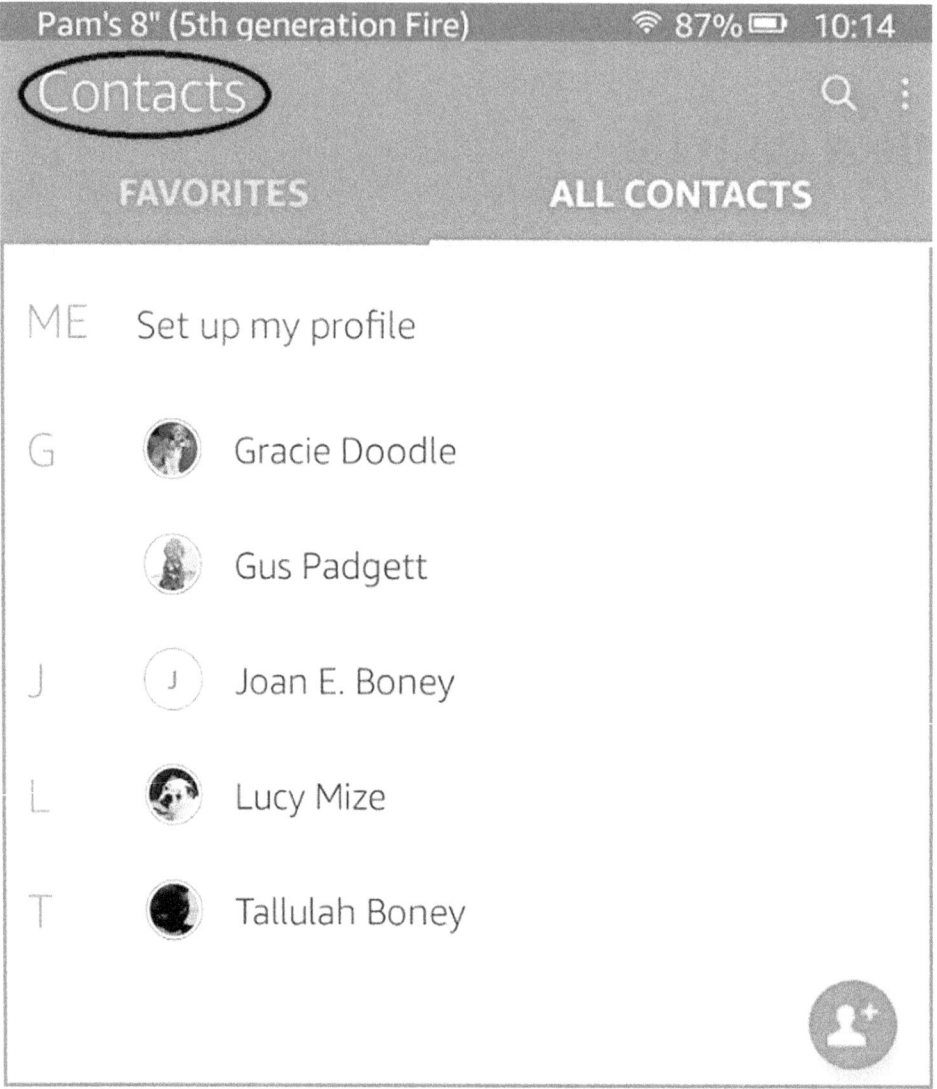

**Tap the name of the contact** you want to edit.

Another screen comes up showing that contact ...

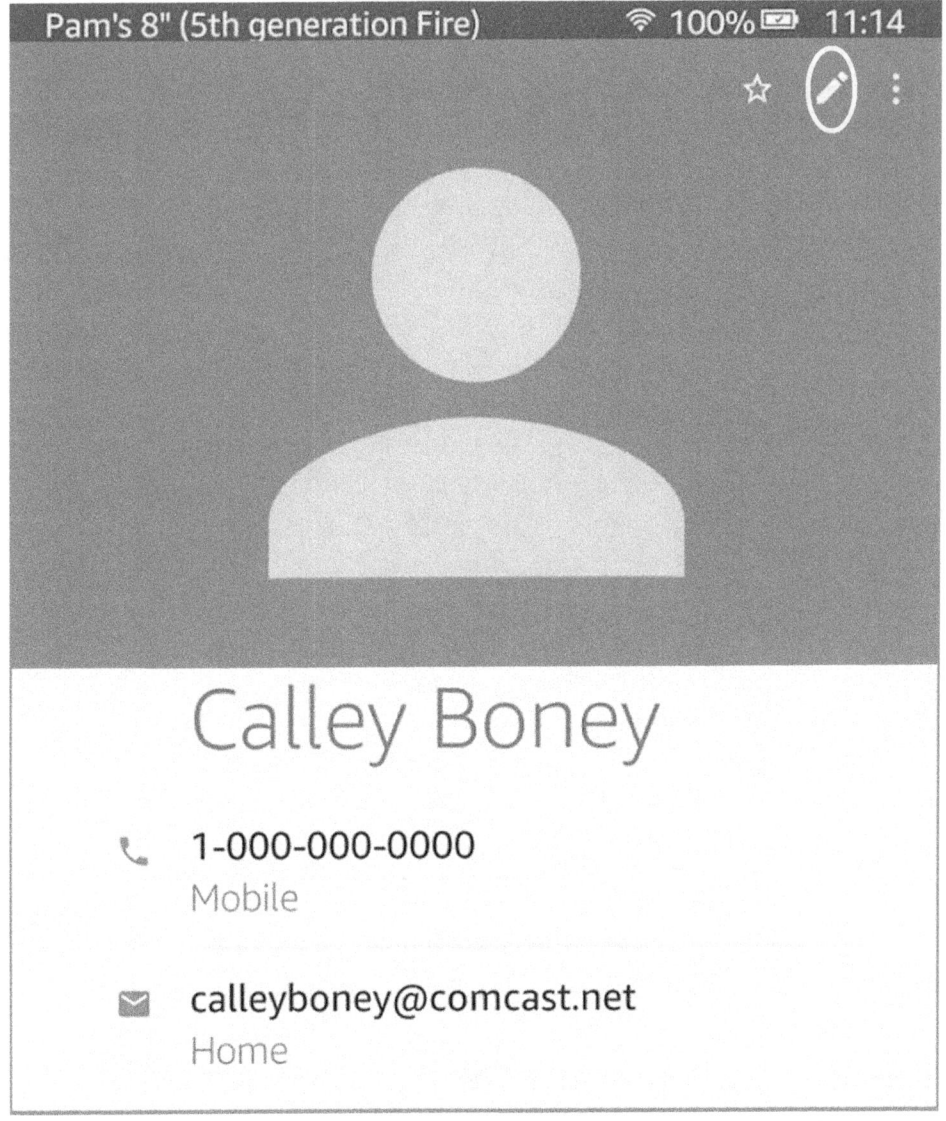

**Tap on the pencil symbol** 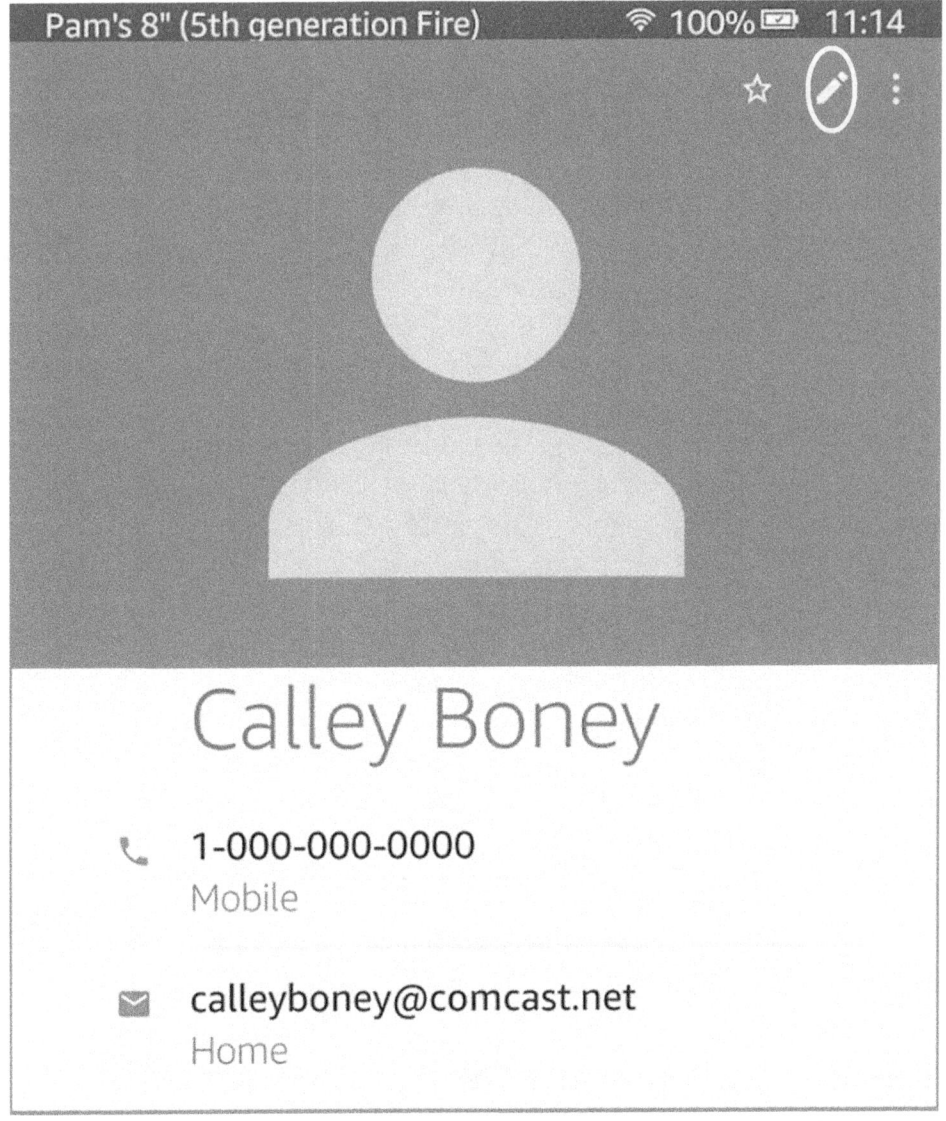 in the top right-hand corner of the screen.

# The Edit Contact screen comes up ...

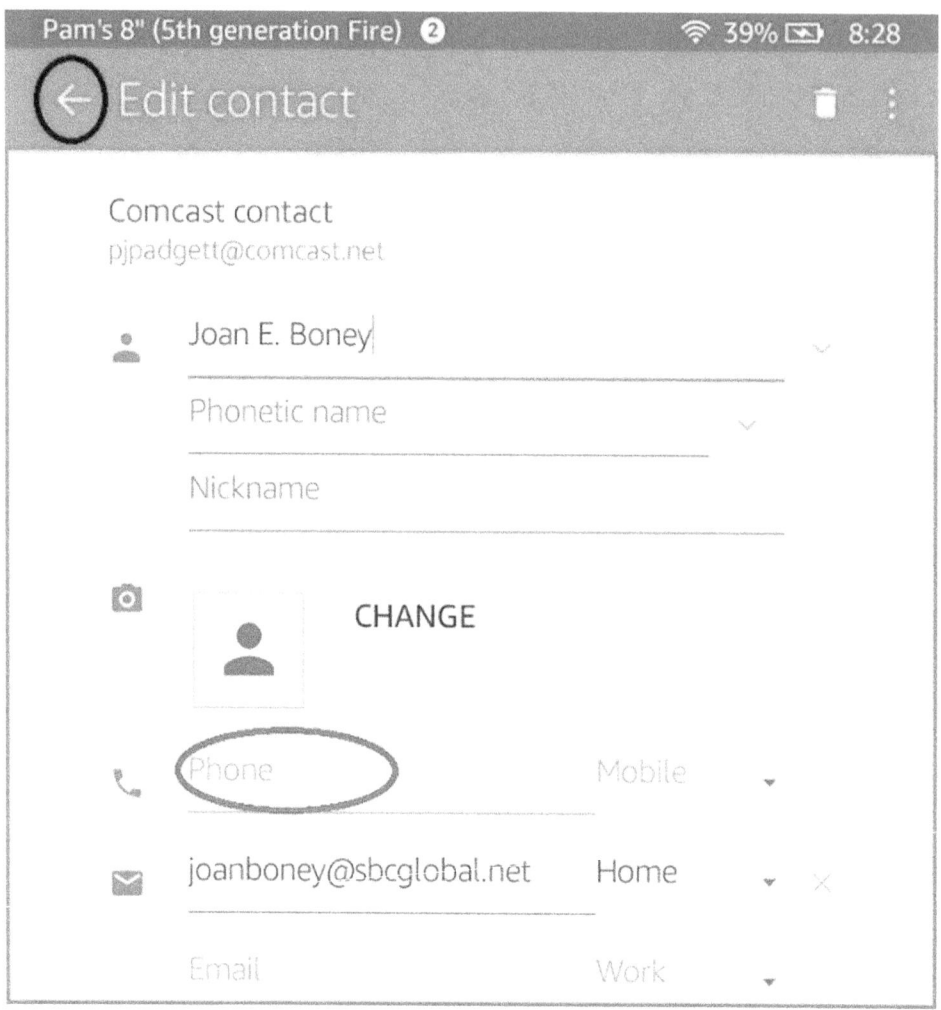

Make any changes you want on the screen. For example, if you want to add a phone number, tap your finger where you see the word "Phone". The keyboard will come up at the bottom of the screen. Using the keyboard, enter the phone number.

**To save the changes, tap on the back arrow**  **in the top left corner of the screen**.

Return to the Home screen by one tap on the circle at bottom of the screen.

## Set A Contact As "Favorite"

To more easily find those persons you contact most frequently, set them up as a "Favorite".

**From the Home screen, tap on the Contacts icon to go to the Contacts screen.**

Contacts

*(You should see a screen with an orange band at the top of the screen with the word "Contacts" on the left side. If another screen comes up, tap the "back" arrow at the bottom of the screen until you get to the screen that says Contacts at the top)*

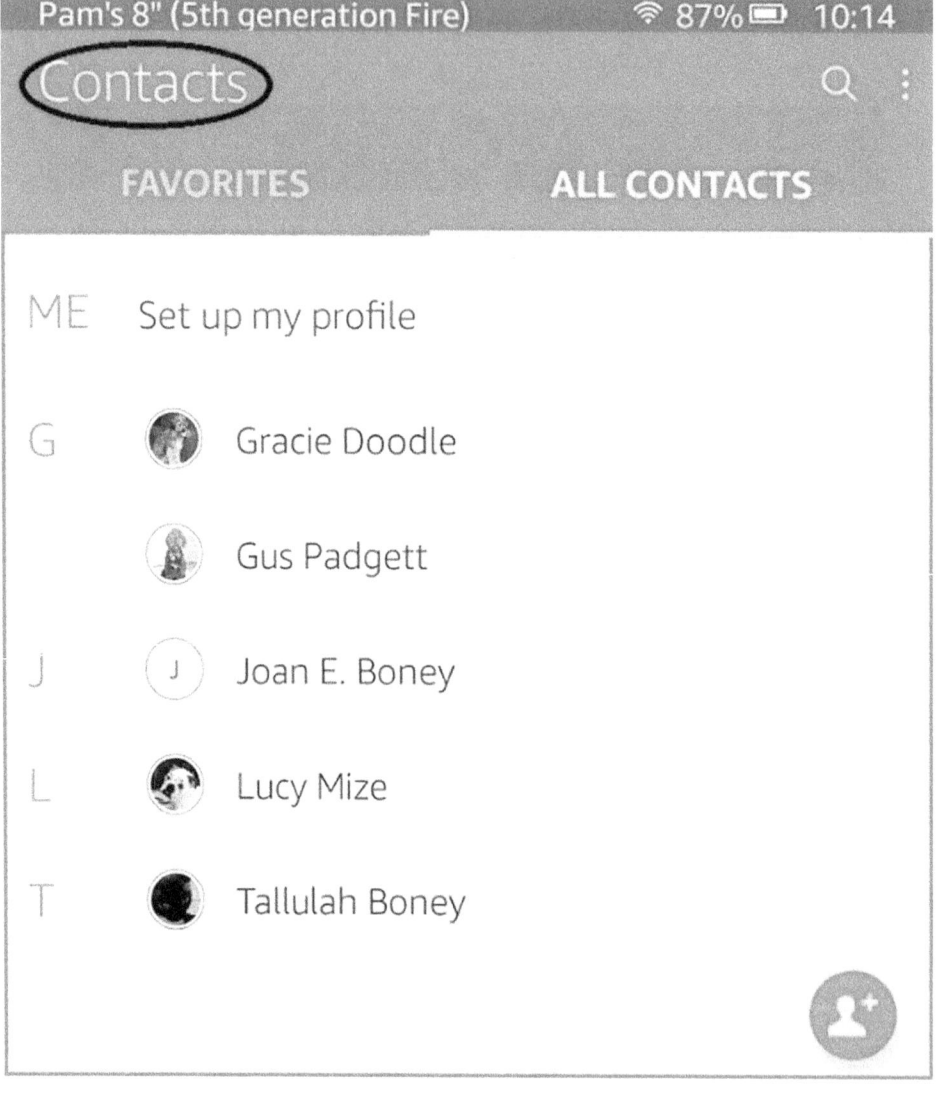

**Tap on the contact you want to make a "Favorite".**

A screen for that contact comes up ...

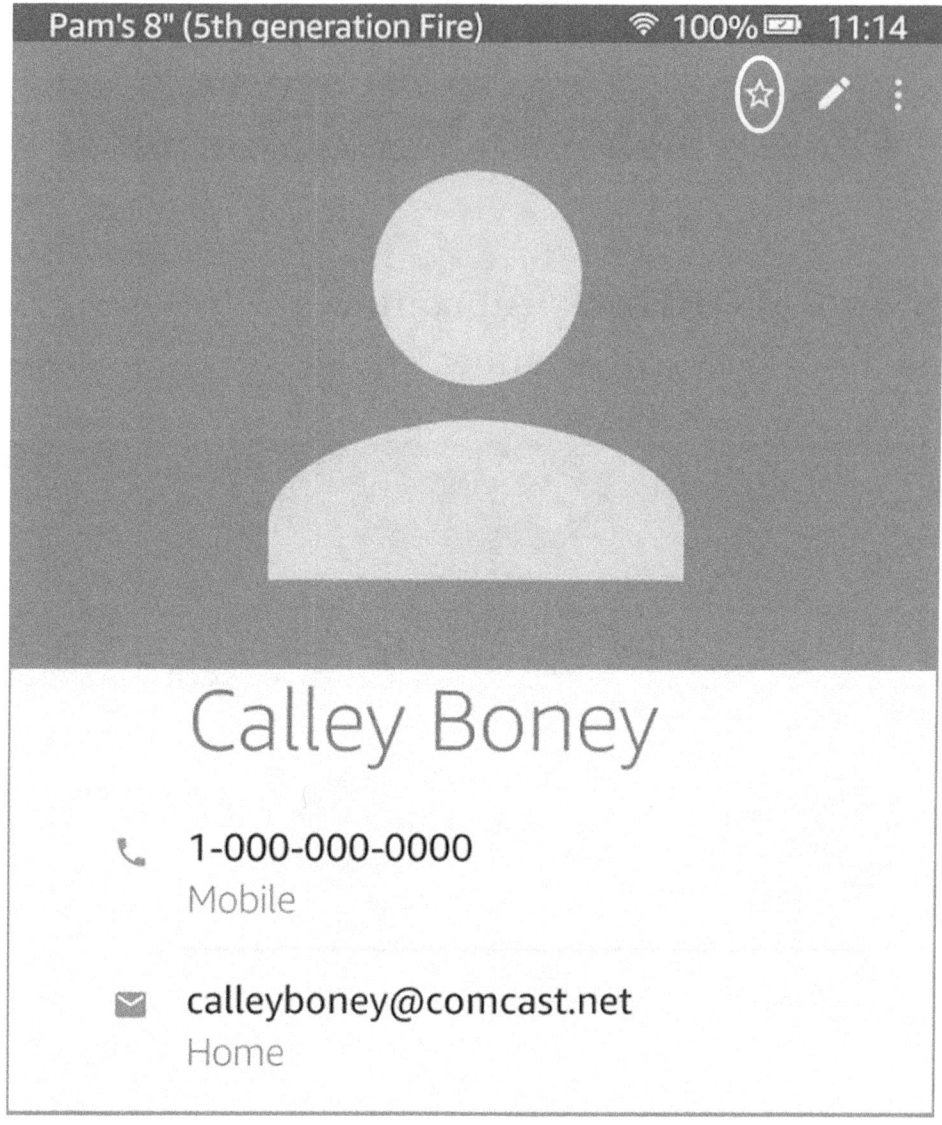

**Tap on the outline of a star** in the upper right corner of the screen.

This contact will now show up on your "Favorites" list.

Tap on "back" arrow at bottom of the screen to go back to the Contacts screen.

**Tap on FAVORITES.** All contacts you have chosen as "Favorites" show up.

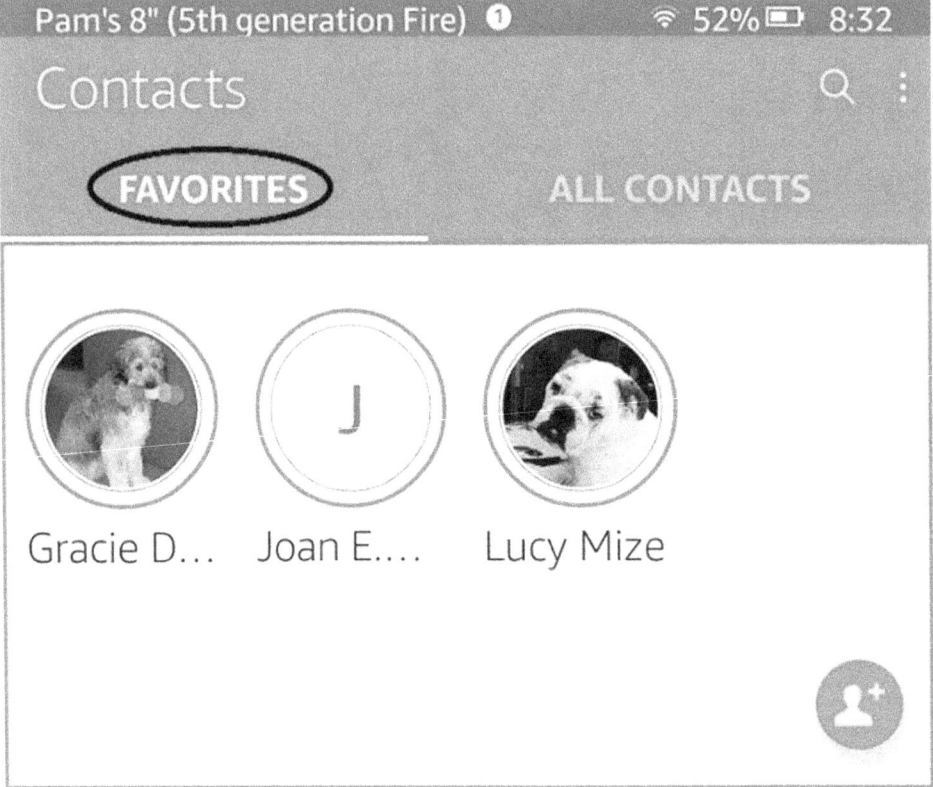

# 9. Emails: Viewing, Replying To, And Forwarding

From Home screen, tap on Email icon

## The Inbox Screen

Make sure you are on your **Inbox screen** by looking at the left side of the blue band at top of the screen.

*(If you are on another email screen, on the left side of the blue band there will be an arrow pointing left.*

***Tap on that arrow until you return to your Inbox Screen.)***

The word "Inbox" should be there.

When you are on the **Inbox Screen**, all current emails on your Kindle will be listed on the screen.

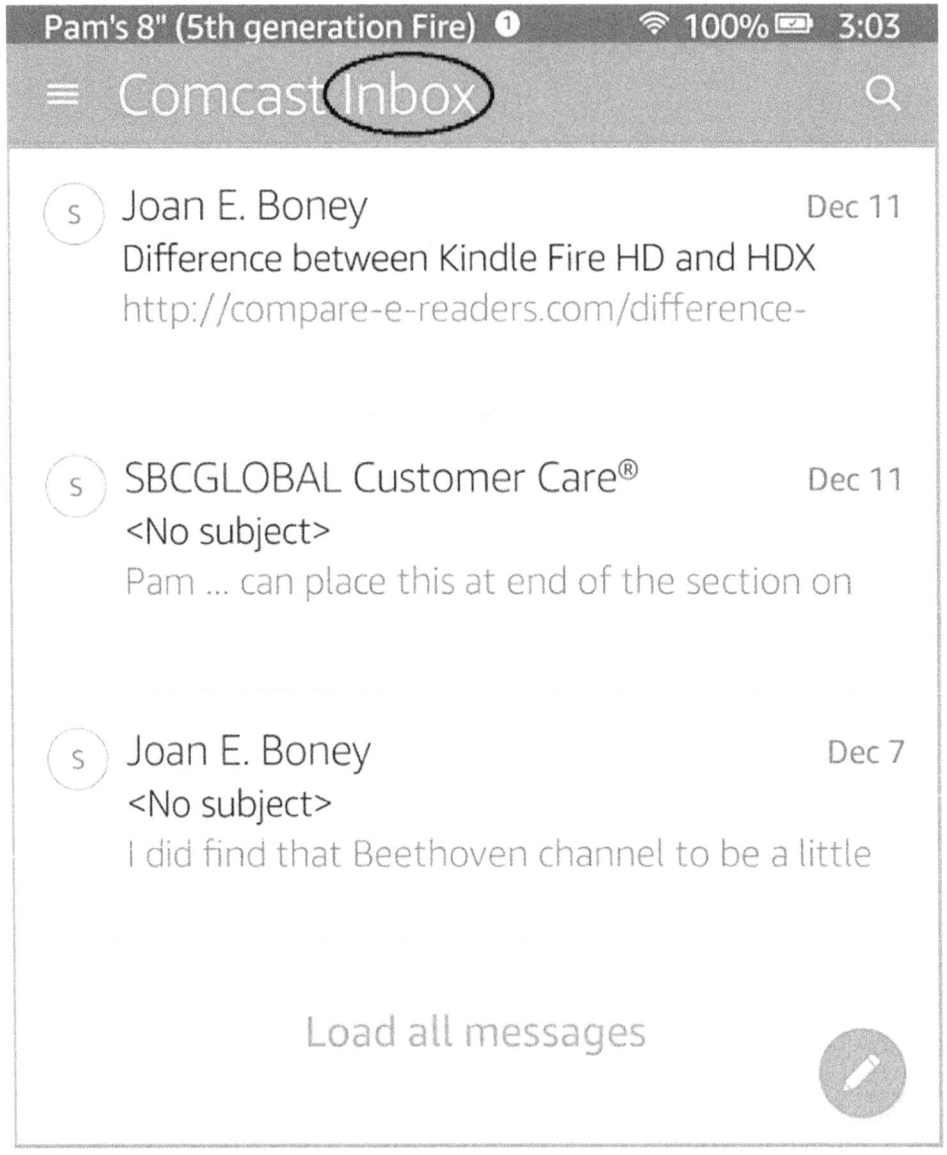

**Tap on email you want to read**. That email will appear on the screen ...

**To return to <u>the Inbox Screen</u>**, tap on the arrow on left side of blue band at top of screen.

# Reply To An Email

After selecting an email from your Inbox, the email will open on your screen.   **There is a curved arrow in the top right corner of the screen ...**

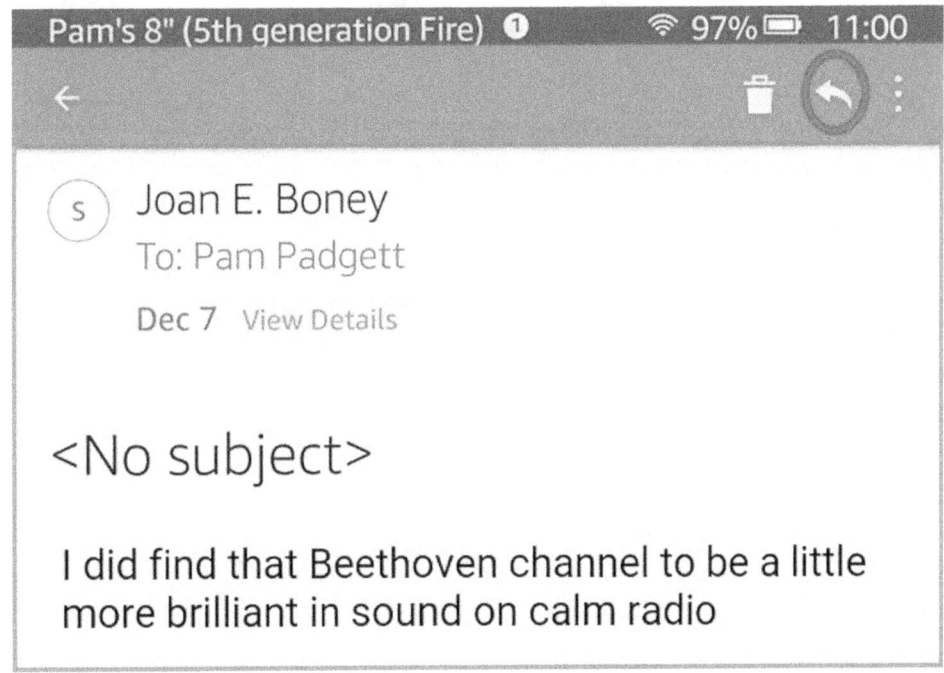

**Tap on the curved arrow.**

The following comes up:

To reply to the email, **tap on Reply.**

An email form displays with the keyboard at the bottom of the screen.

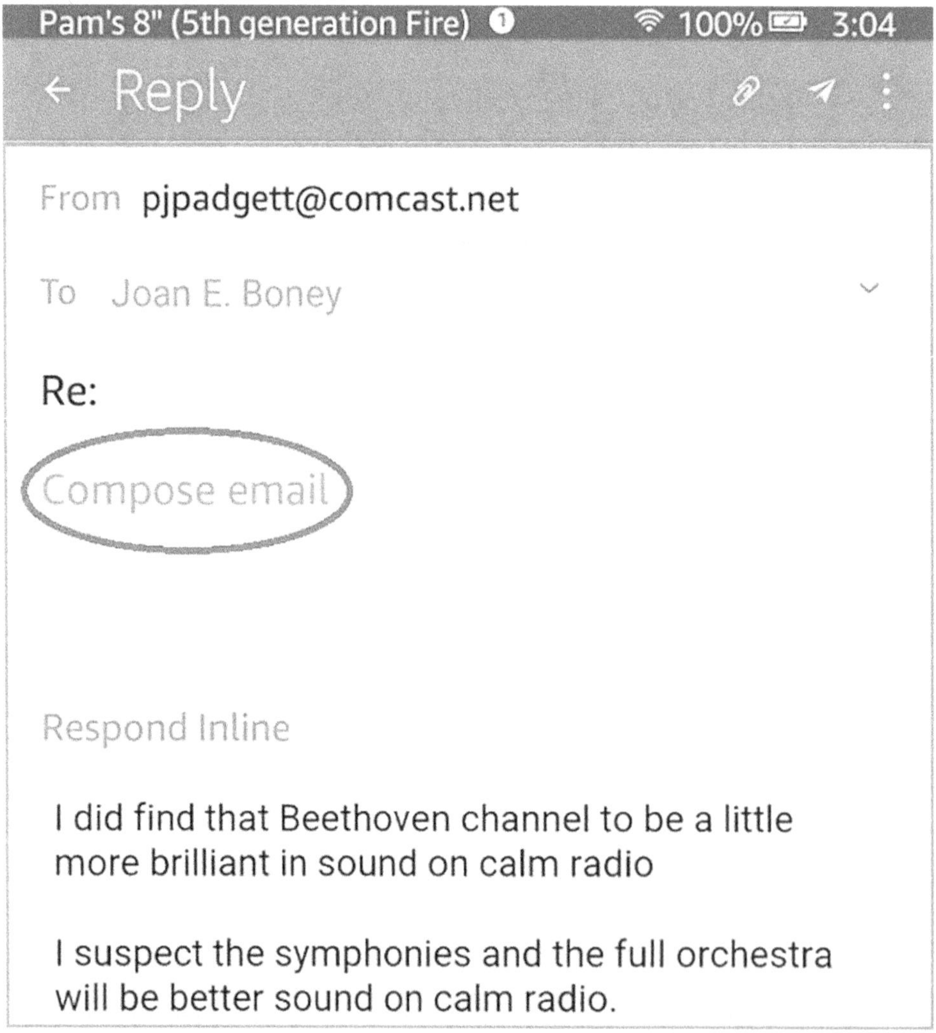

Pam's 8" (5th generation Fire) ❶          📶 100% 🔋 3:04

← Reply                          🔗 ✈ ⋮

From  pjpadgett@comcast.net

To    Joan E. Boney                              ⌄

Re:

Compose email

Respond Inline

I did find that Beethoven channel to be a little more brilliant in sound on calm radio

I suspect the symphonies and the full orchestra will be better sound on calm radio.

**Tap where you see "Compose email" and write your response.**

**Send your response by tapping on the symbol**

**that looks like a paper airplane**  in the top right of the screen.

## Forward An Email

After selecting an email from your Inbox, the email will open on your screen. **There is a curved arrow in the top right corner of the screen** ...

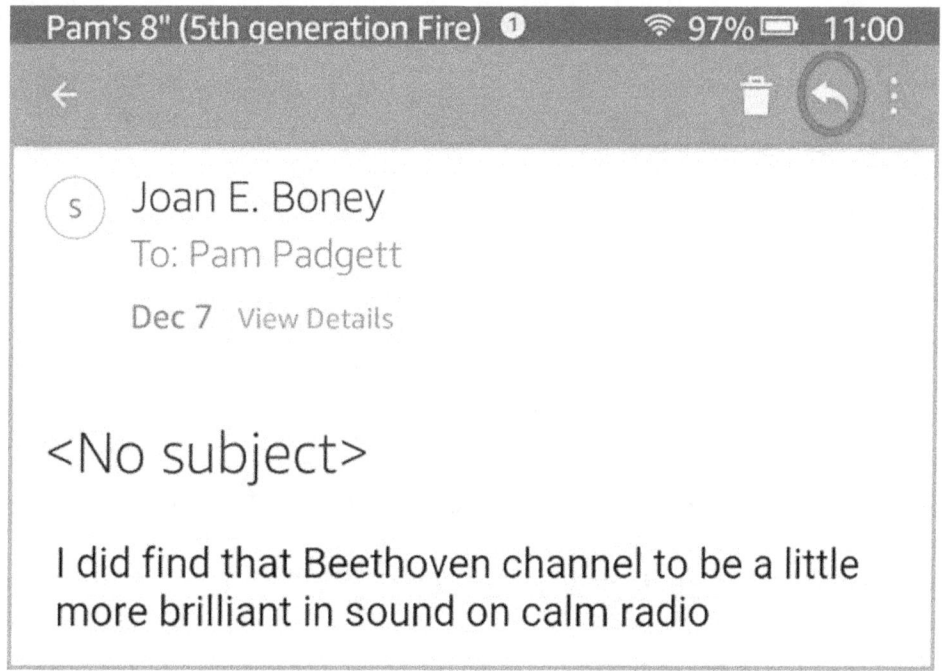

## Tap on the curved arrow.

A list comes up:

## Tap on <u>forward.</u>

The following comes on screen ...

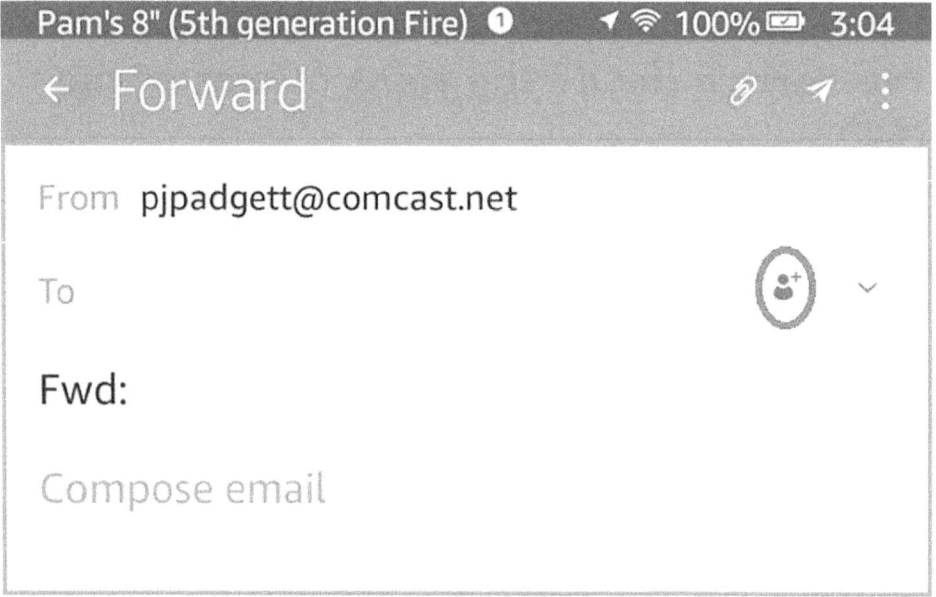

Tap on the symbol that looks like a person on right side of the screen on the "To" line.

This pulls up your list of Contacts ...

**<u>Tap on the name of the person</u>** to whom you wish to forward the email.

The email "To" will show that person.

(If you wish to send the email to more than one person, tap on the 👤 figure again. This will allow you to select another person from your contact list.)

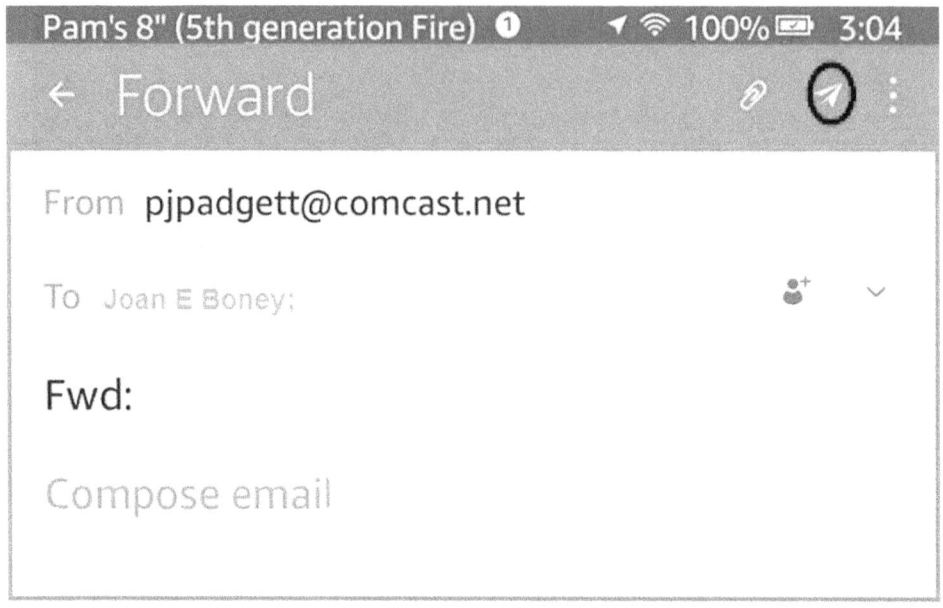

You can then tap where you see "**Compose email**" to write a response, if you wish.

**Send your response by tapping on the symbol that looks like a paper airplane** 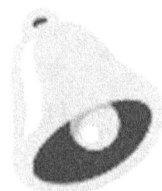 in the top right of the screen.

**Refresh Inbox (Bring In New Emails)**

Emails usually come to your email Inbox automatically. If you want to manually check for any new emails, you can ...

**Put your finger below blue band at top of screen**.

**Make a quick swiping motion down the screen**.

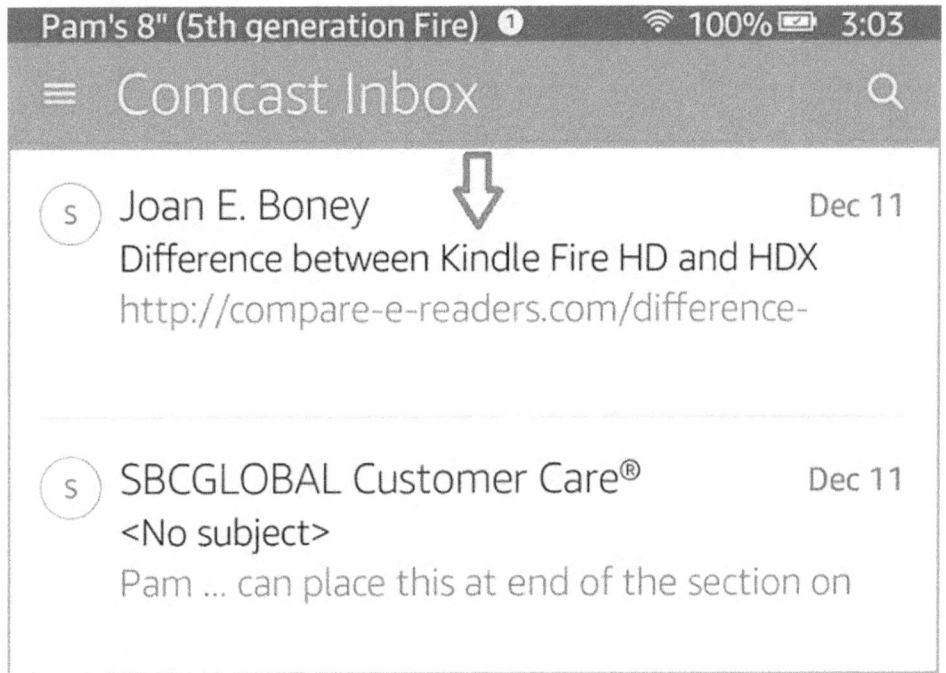

# 10. Emails: Creating And Deleting

## Create An Email

### From Home screen, tap on Email icon:

Make sure you are on your **Inbox screen** by looking at the left side of the blue band at top of the screen.    The word "Inbox" should be there.

(*If you are on another email screen, on the left side of the blue band there will be an arrow pointing left.*

***Tap on that arrow until you return to your Inbox Screen.***)

## On the Inbox screen, tap on the pencil

at bottom right corner of the screen.

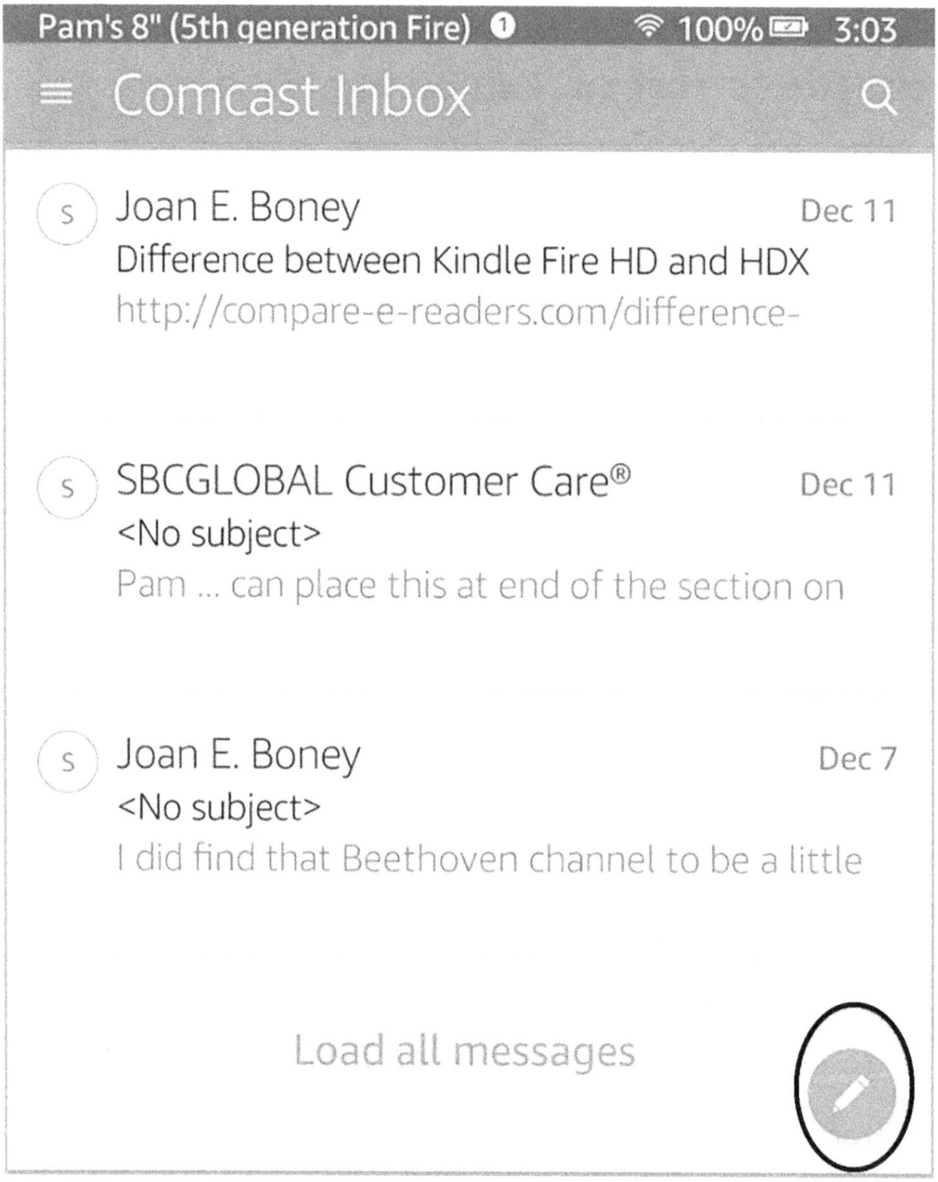

Pam's 8" (5th generation Fire) ❶          📶 100% 🔋 3:03

≡  Comcast Inbox                                    Q

ⓢ  Joan E. Boney                                Dec 11
    Difference between Kindle Fire HD and HDX
    http://compare-e-readers.com/difference-

ⓢ  SBCGLOBAL Customer Care®                Dec 11
    <No subject>
    Pam ... can place this at end of the section on

ⓢ  Joan E. Boney                                 Dec 7
    <No subject>
    I did find that Beethoven channel to be a little

                    Load all messages

A new email form will display with a keyboard below it ...

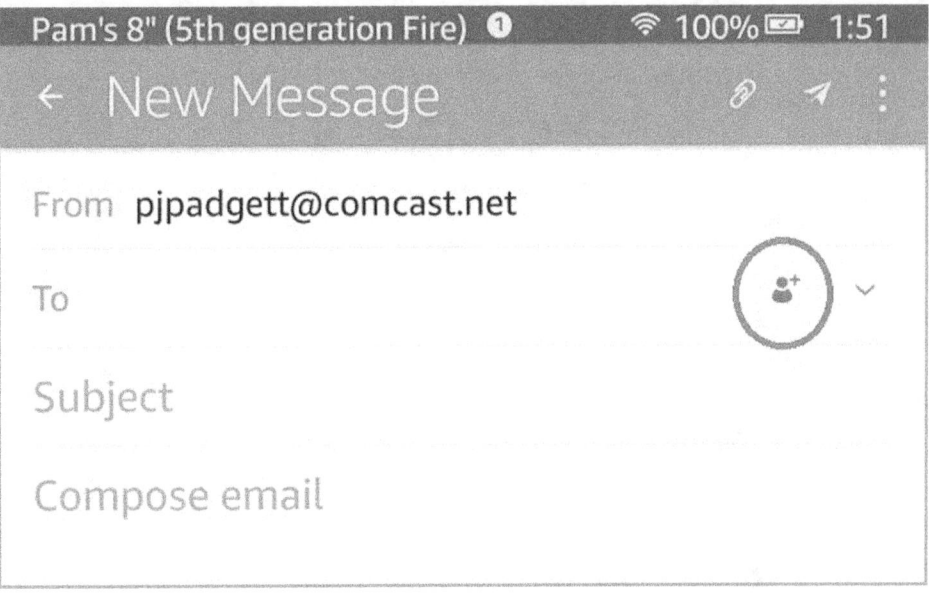

**From:** your email address will already be filled in.

**To:** enter person(s) you want to send email to by one tap on the symbol that looks like a person on right side of the screen.

This pulls up your list of Contacts ....

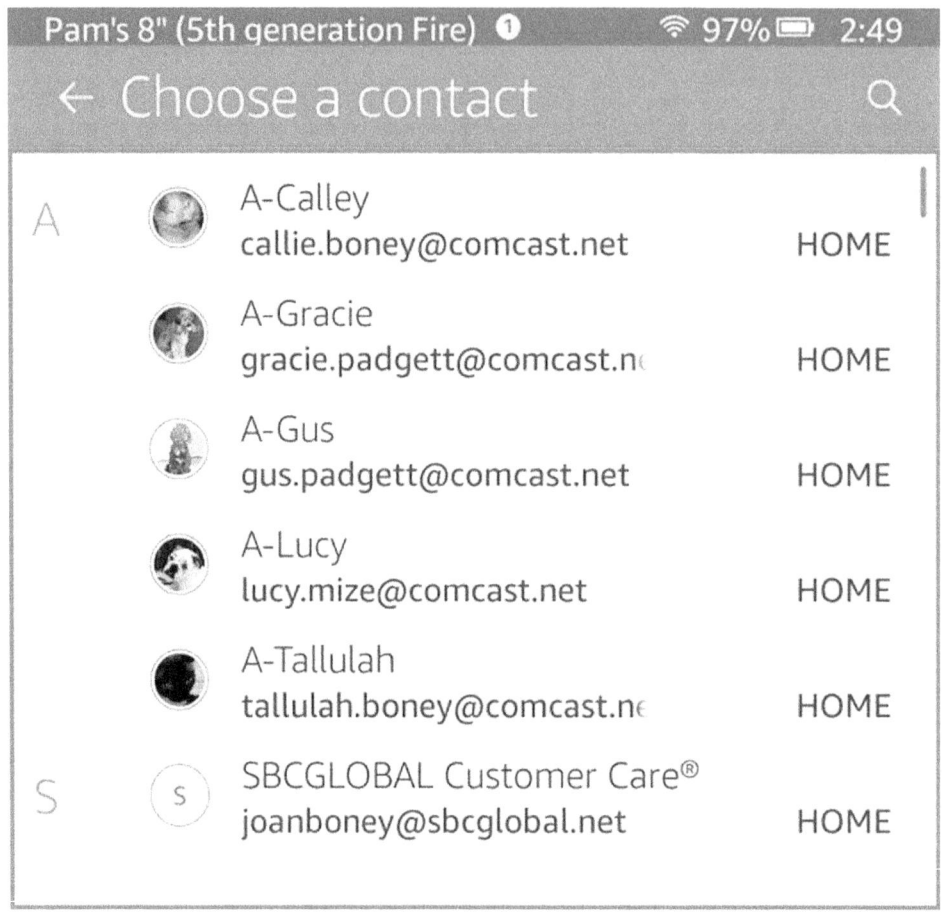

**Tap on the person(s)** you want to send the email to. The email form will again come up.

If you want to send the email to another person, tap on the 👤⁺ symbol again. The name for each person will be on the **To**: line.

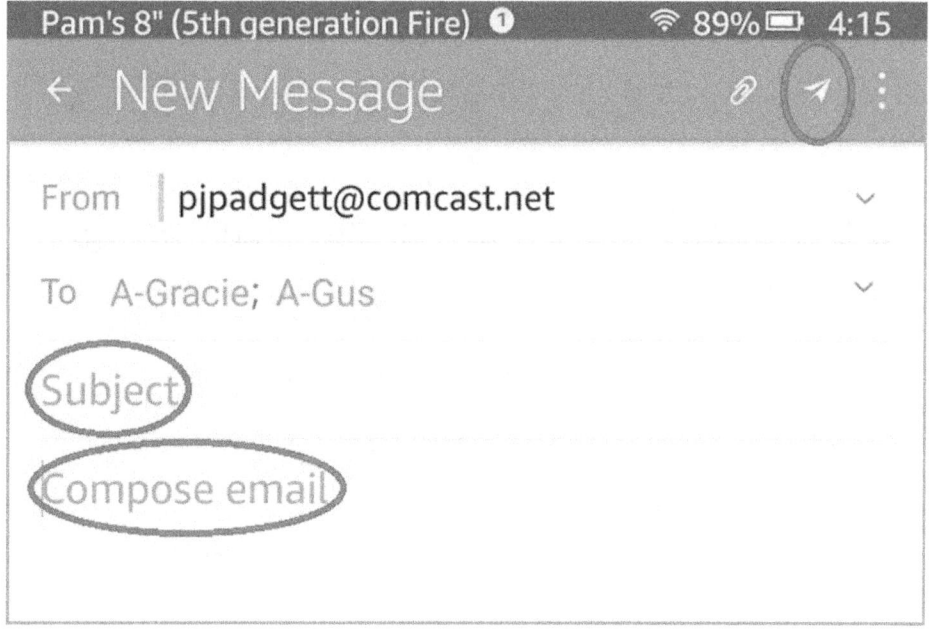

**Subject:** tap here to enter a subject, if you choose

**Compose email.** tap here to write your email.

**Send your email by tapping on the symbol that looks like a paper airplane**  in the top right of the screen.

# Delete Email You Are Viewing

From the Inbox, tap on an email. This brings it onto the screen.

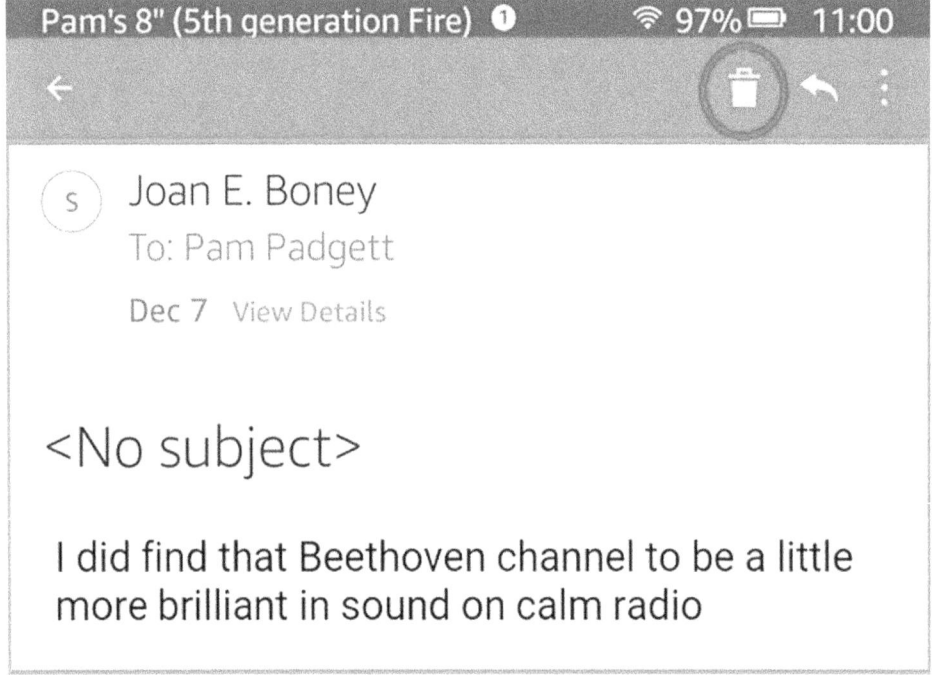

**Tap the trash can** at top right of the screen.

The email will be deleted and the Inbox will come up.

# Delete Multiple Emails

On the Inbox screen, there are circles with a letter or picture to the left of each email.

**Tap in the circle of each email you want to delete**. A check mark is now in the circle.

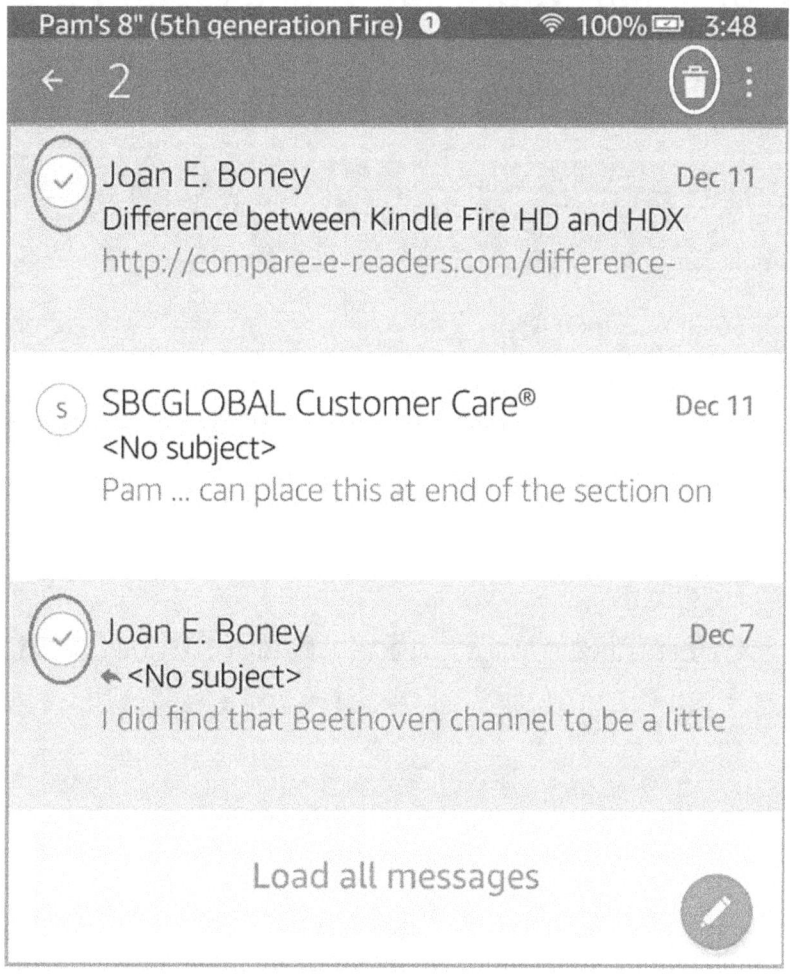

**Tap on the trash can** in the top right corner of the screen. Each email with a check mark will be deleted.

## Delete Emails One At A Time From Inbox

On the Inbox screen, hold your finger at the right edge of an email you want to delete, and drag your finger toward the left side of the screen. That email will be deleted.

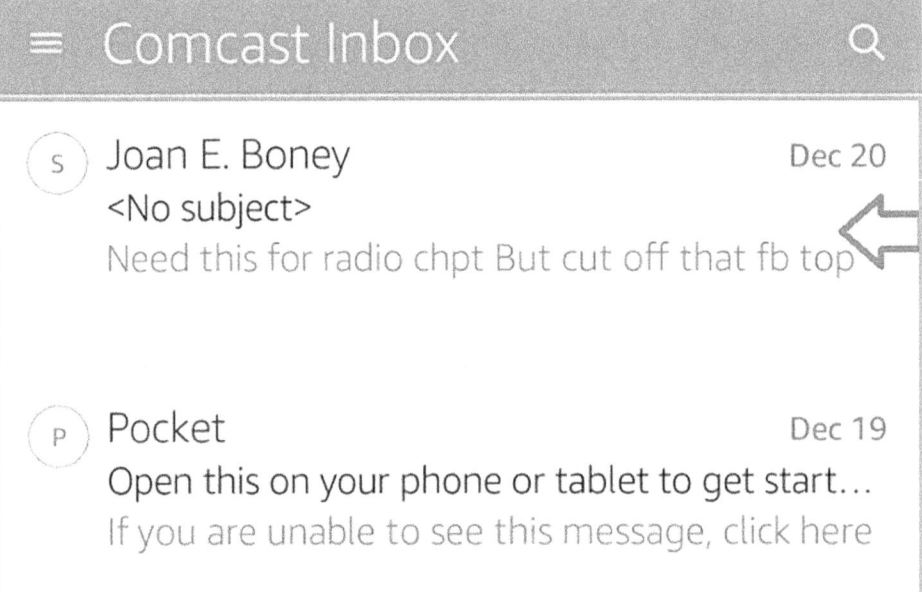

# 11. Books

## Order Book From Amazon Shop

From the Home Page: Tap on the **"Amazon <u>Shop</u>"** icon.

This takes you directly to the Amazon store.

**A search window** appears at top of screen.

**Tap on the search window** and a keyboard will pop up at bottom of screen.

Type in **author's name <u>"in Kindle"</u>**.

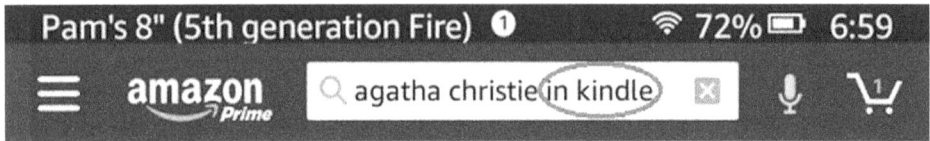

*(Be sure to put <u>"in Kindle"</u> on the search screen after author's name. You can also type name of book in the search box but again, be sure to put <u>"in Kindle"</u> otherwise it will sometimes bring up paper books which you might order by mistake.)*

**Click on <u>the yellow circle</u> at bottom of your keyboard**.

A list of books written by that author will appear on screen ...

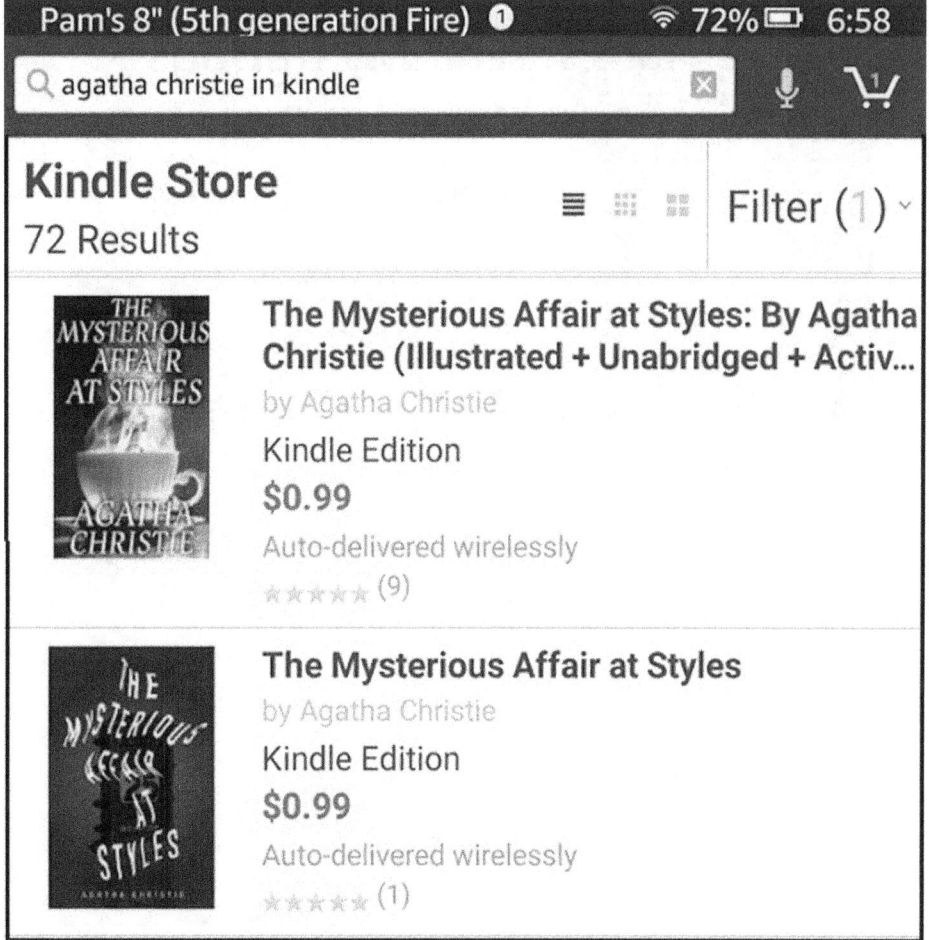

**Tap** on book you want to view.

You will see: **Download sample** *( free) or* **Buy ...**

**Tap on your choice.**

The book will automatically begin to download onto your Kindle and you can begin reading in seconds by single tap on the book in your **Book Section** of Kindle... **or on your home page ...**

*(Sometimes "new" books / newly ordered / newly downloaded books, will appear on home page above icons ... Newly ordered books <u>always</u> appear in BOOKS, just tap BOOKS, in Carousel.)*

## Bookmarks

### <u>Add Bookmark:</u>

**Tap in the top right-hand corner of the page you want to bookmark**. A bookmark symbol ▐ will <u>usually</u> appear where you tap.

If the bookmark symbol ▐ does not appear in the top-right-hand corner of the page, you can set a bookmark by doing the following steps:

**Tap one time in the center of the page**. The following will show up at the top of the screen ...

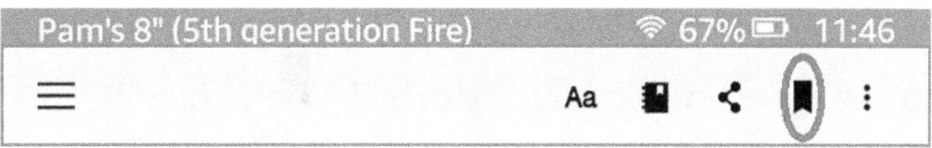

## Tap on the bookmark symbol

A screen will come down in upper right corner:

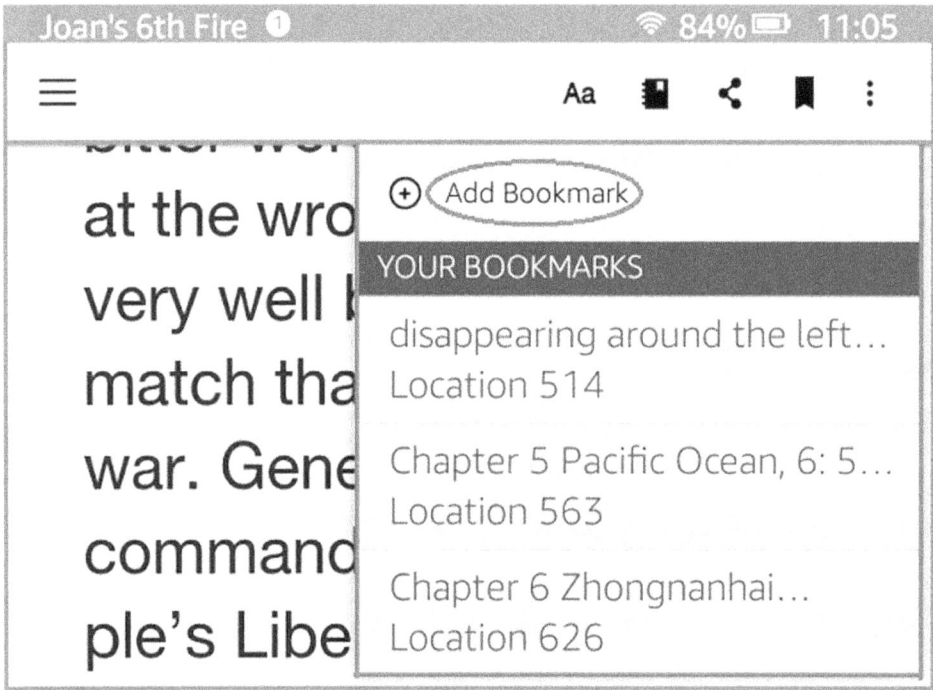

## Tap on the plus sign

This will cause that page, **where you are currently reading,** to be bookmarked.

## Remove a bookmark from a page

## Tap on the bookmark symbol ▮. It will usually disappear.

If the bookmark symbol is still on the book page, you can remove it by doing the following steps:

**Tap one time in the center of the page.** The following will show up at the top of the screen ...

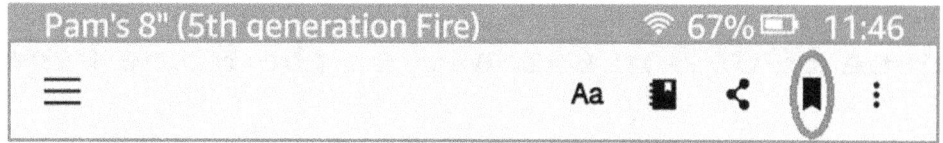

**Tap on the bookmark symbol** ▐

A screen will come down in upper right corner:

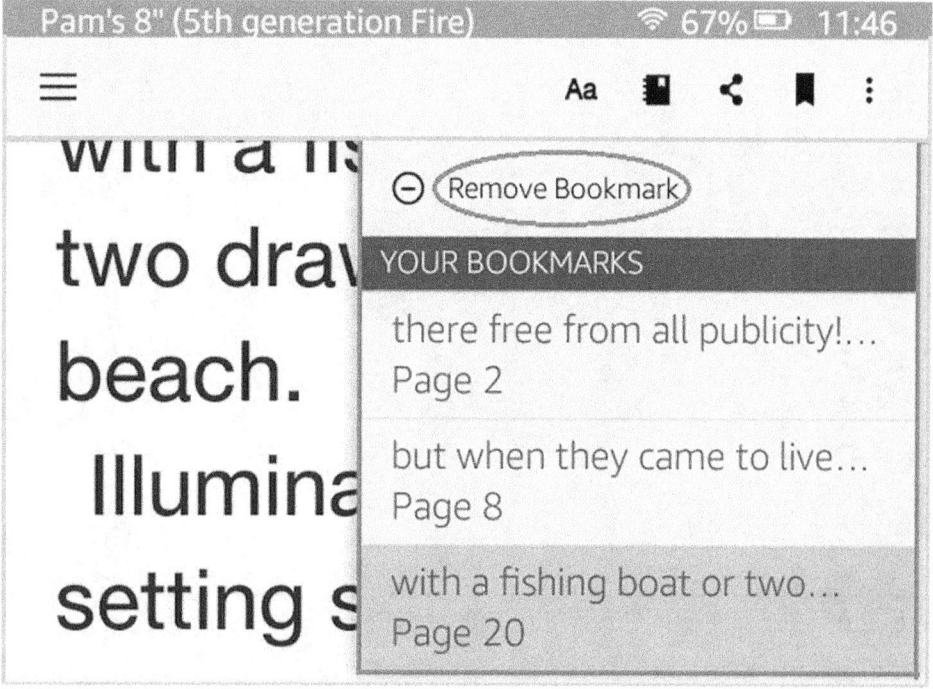

**Tap on the minus sign.**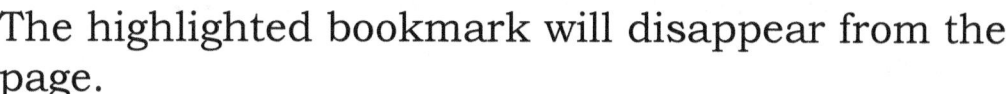

The highlighted bookmark will disappear from the page.

# Remove Book From Your Active Library

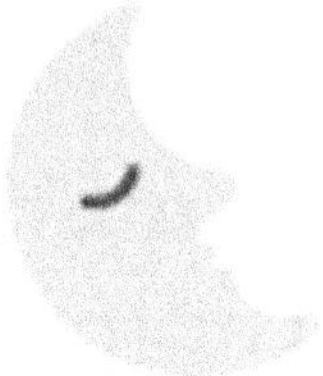

## Tap on BOOKS in Carousel on the Home Page.

![Books library screenshot showing Search Books, BOOKS VIDEO GA LIBRARY STORE, FROM YOUR BOOKS LIBRARY with The Mysterious... by Christie, Agatha, and See all of your books]

**Tap "See all of your books" at the bottom of the section titled "FROM YOUR BOOKS LIBRARY".**

On the next screen that comes up, **tap on DOWNLOADED.**

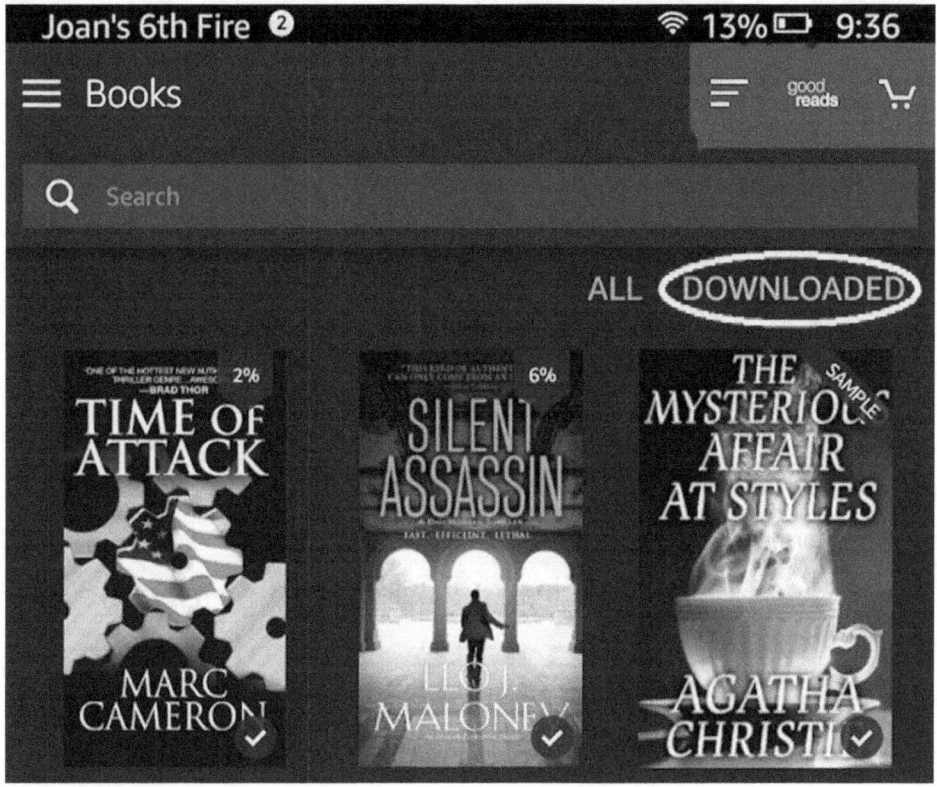

With finger, press down <u>and hold on center of the book</u> that is to be removed, until a check mark appears on center of book.

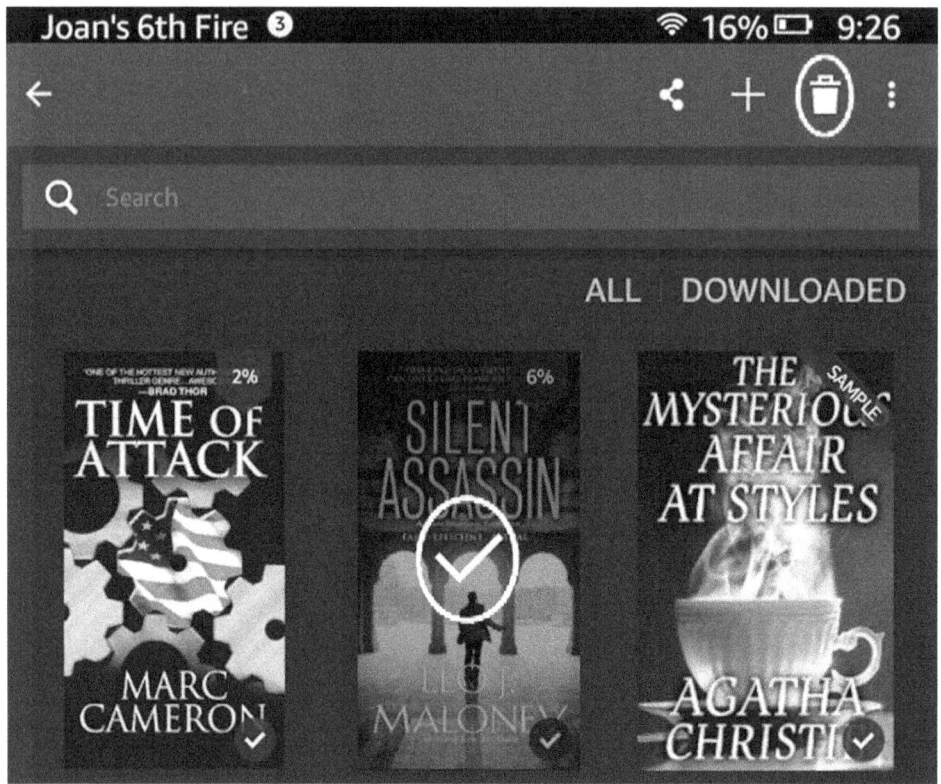

**After check mark appears <u>in center of book</u>, tap the <u>trash can</u> on upper right of screen.** Book will leave the screen.

**Another way to remove book and send book to storage library is when you hold down on center of book cover on book you want to remove, a small menu will come up saying" remove from home" / "remove from device". I tap "remove from device." If the book remains on my book shelf, then I hold finger down again on center of book and when another choice screen appears for me to "remove"**

**book, I tap on that "remove" choice and book vanishes from my active book shelf.**

*(The book has gone to cloud storage. You can retrieve that book by one tap on the "All" setting beside the "Download" setting on your BOOK page.)*

**<u>All</u> means "all books in your total library"** (including those you have sent to cloud storage)

**<u>Downloaded</u> are those active books on your book shelf.**

# Retrieve Book From Storage And Return To Library

**Go to your BOOK library.  Tap on "ALL".**

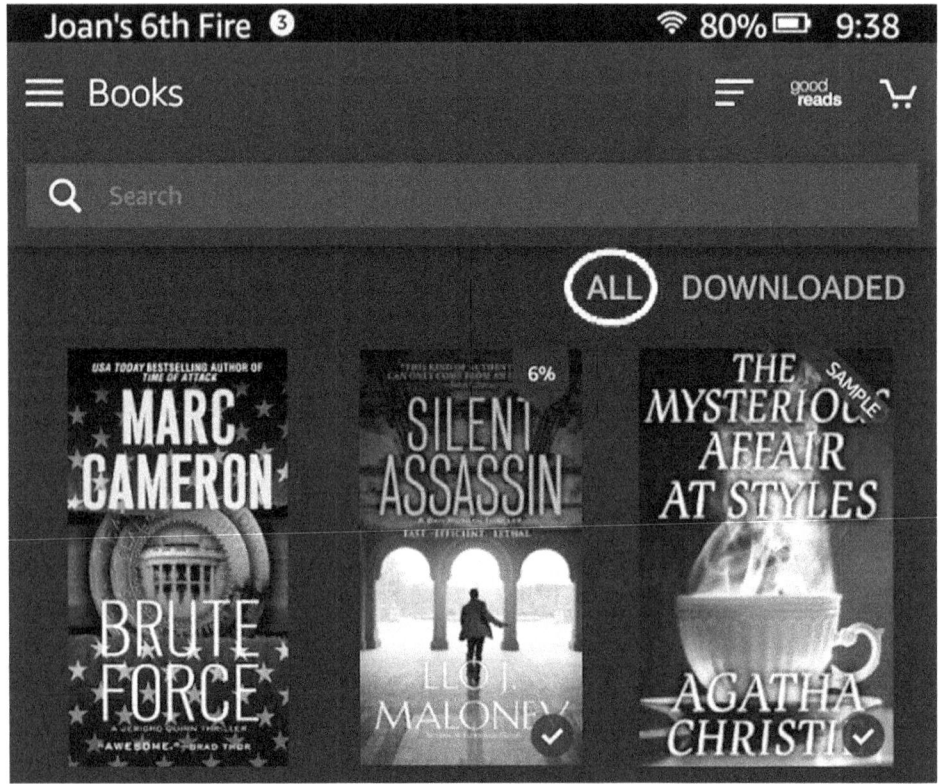

**This puts you into your storage library.**

**To download a book, (returning book to your active library shelf), tap on lower <u>right</u> corner of book cover.**

An "x" will appear and you will see a yellow line moving under the "x".

The book is downloading to your "Downloaded file".

The book is now on your active library shelf. You will see a check mark appear where the "x" had been.  <u>This means the book is downloaded and ready to read.</u>

Tap one time on the cover of the book to open the book.

The book will remain downloaded (on your active book shelf) until you choose to remove the book and put it back into "storage"

# 12. Internet

The internet, or "the web", is like a highway system that goes all over the world.

There are stores, such as **Amazon**, where we can view and purchase merchandise.

There are **encyclopedias**, such as **Wikipedia**, where we can receive information about many subjects and people.

There are **blogs** where information is shared.

The Internet is **"The World Wide Web"**.  Each location is called "a web site."

Each web site  has a **"web address"**.

**Amazon's** address is **www.amazon.com**.

*(The web address is sometimes referred to as a* **URL***.  When you see URL on your Kindle, that is the same as a web address).*

On the Kindle Fire, the **Silk Browser** is the way we get to the internet.  *(There are multiple browsers.  Amazon uses a browser called "Silk".)*

From the Home screen, tap on the **Silk Browser** icon:

The **Silk Browser** opens.

Let's start at the Silk Home screen.  Tap on the ♠ symbol and you'll see the Silk Home screen.

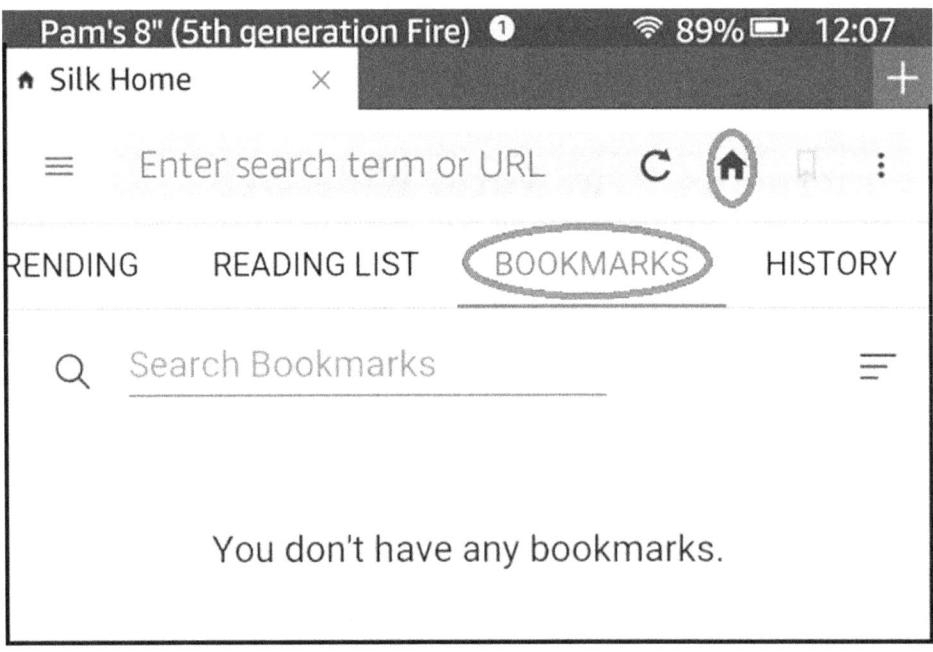

**Tap on BOOKMARKS  under the Search Box.**

**This is very important.  You will see 5 optional settings located under the Search Box** (see *above graphic).*

**These words take you to other screens under the Silk Home page.**

**MOST VISITED ... TRENDING ... READING LIST ... <u>BOOKMARK</u> ... HISTORY***(one of these 5 will be underlined)*

While you might look at these settings, we are encouraging you to keep the **<u>Silk Home</u>** set on the **BOOKMARK** setting. If you will do that, you will find it significantly easier to use a search box to get to other locations, and you will be able to keep an uncluttered BOOKMARK page to help you return to favorite web sites with minimum effort.

**(When Silk Home is set on <u>BOOKMARK</u> a line will always appear under the word "<u>BOOKMARK</u>".)**

## Use Search To Get To A Web-Site

**Now we are going to find an Internet site to order a Pizza.**

## There is a grey box across the top of the screen where it says:  <u>Enter search term or URL</u>  *(a "search box")*

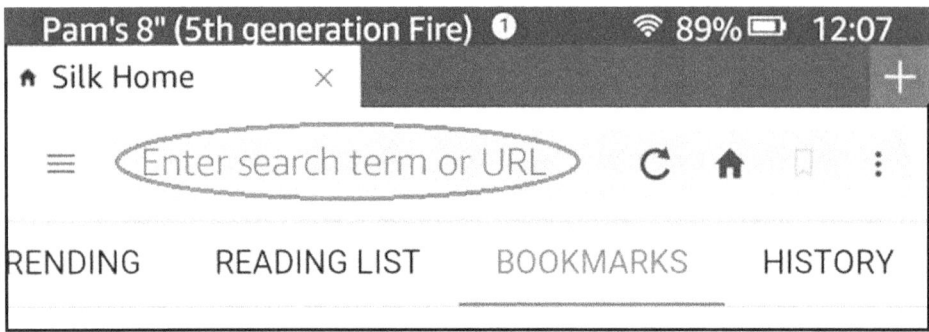

**Tap inside that box** and a keyboard will appear on the lower portion of your screen.  You will see a line blinking in front of the word "Enter" ... (that blinking line is called a cursor.

Let's order the "Pizza" ... If you **type PIZZA into your Search Box**, and you live in Colorado Springs, the following will appear on your screen:

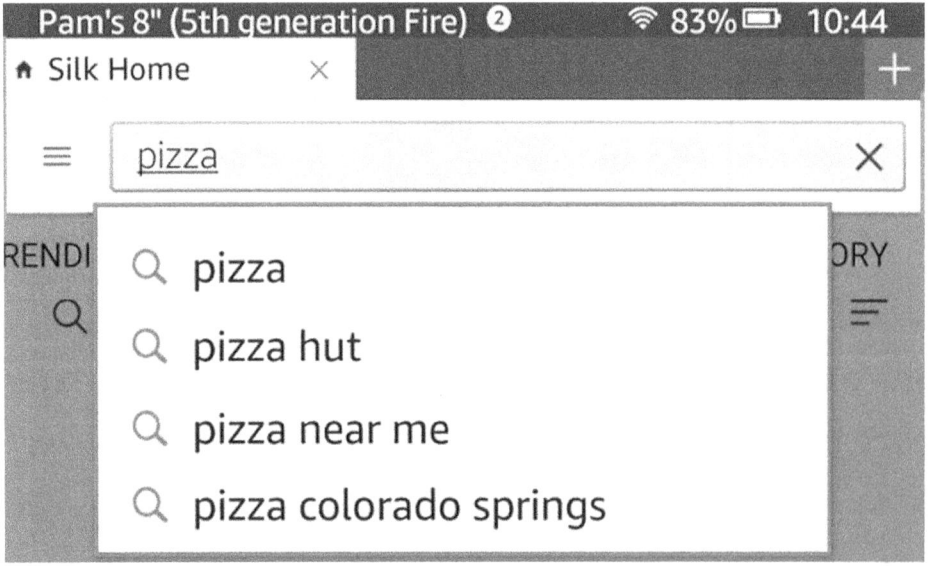

**Tap on pizza.**

A screen will come up giving you options.

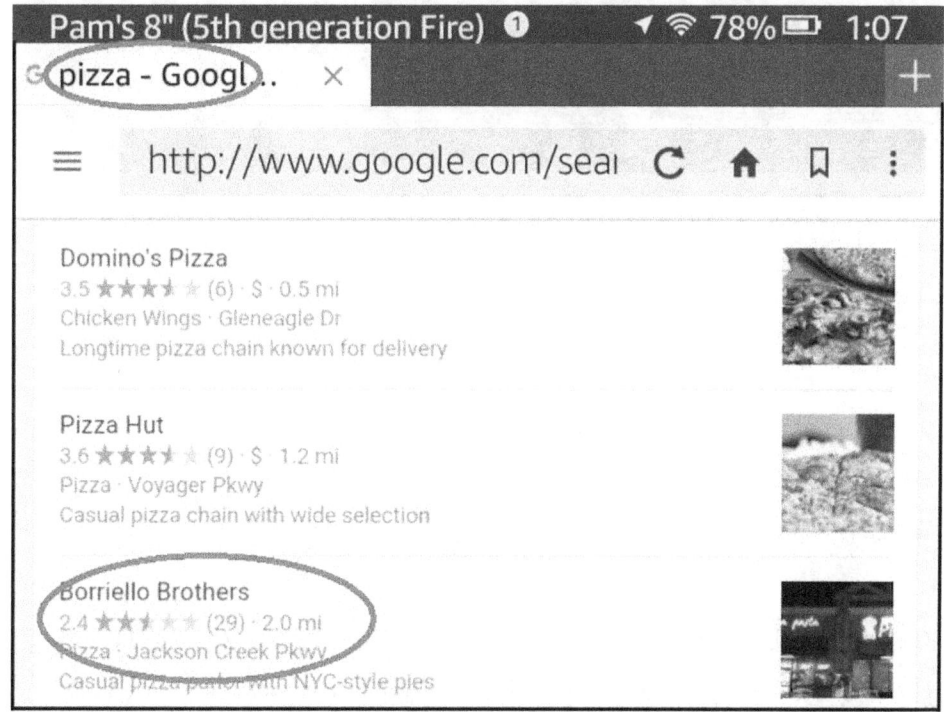

**Tap on the option of your choice,** the name of the pizza place where you want to order your pizza.

**A tab will have automatically appeared at the top of your screen, saying "Pizza". You'll see the web site for the selected pizza shop on the screen.**

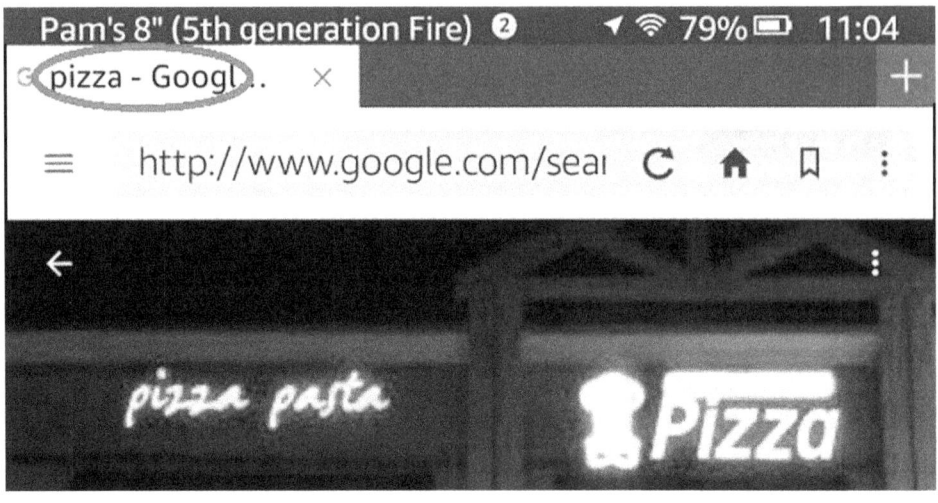

## Bookmarks

If you frequently order pizza, you may want to make **a bookmark** on the pizza screen so you can easily get back to this pizza web site.

The □ symbol in the top right area of the screen is a bookmark symbol. Tap on that symbol to bookmark the Pizza shop.

**The bookmark symbol will turn black when the web site has been bookmarked.**

**Each place you have "<u>bookmarked</u>" will appear on the Silk Home <u>Bookmarks</u> screen**.  Once you have bookmarked a web site, you can easily get back to it from the Silk Home Bookmarks screen.

<u>(Remember, to get to the Silk Home screen tap on the</u> 🏠 <u>symbol</u>.  On the Silk Home screen tap on BOOKMARKS so that it is underlined)

Now you can tap on any of the bookmarks listed.

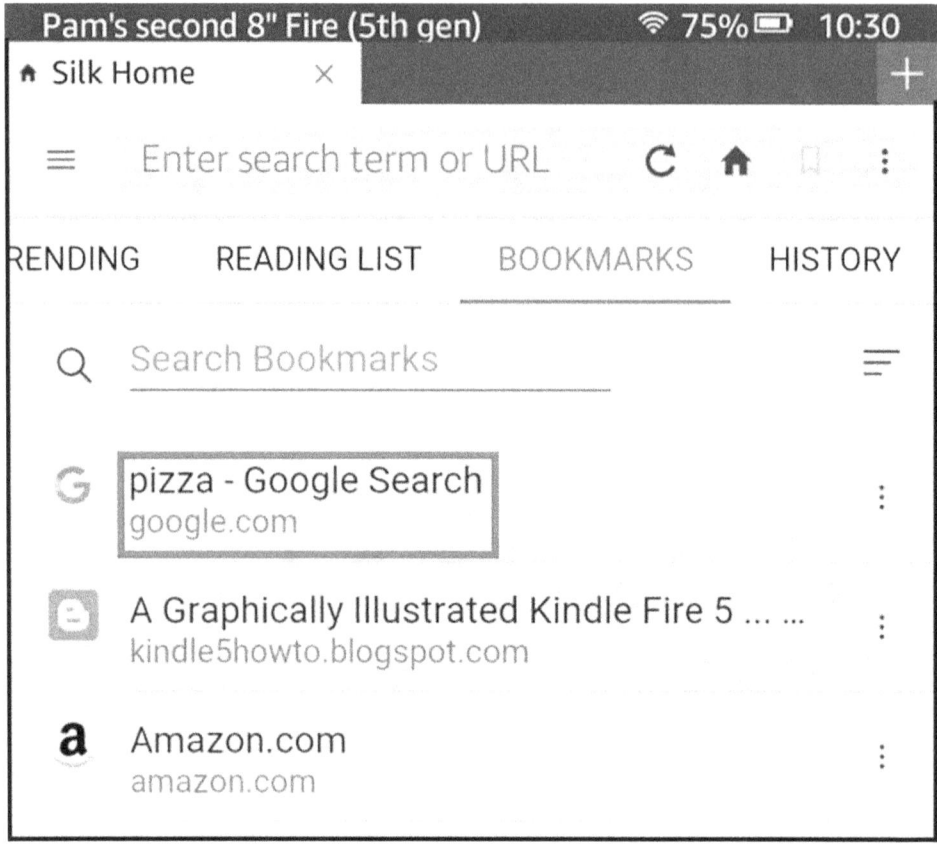

**If you want to remove the bookmark,** just tap on the bookmark in the list of bookmarks. The screen for that web site will come up. **Tap on the bookmark symbol**

The bookmark will become just outlined showing that the bookmark has been removed.

# Create Multiple Tabs (Switching Between Internet Sites)

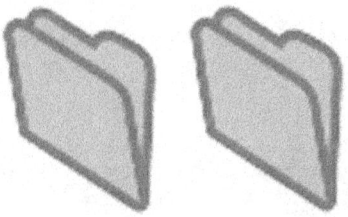

**At the top right hand corner of your screen you will see a plus "+" symbol.**

**Tap on the plus "+" sign ...**

This brings up a new Silk Home screen. **Now we have two tabs at the top of the page, Pizza and Silk Home.**

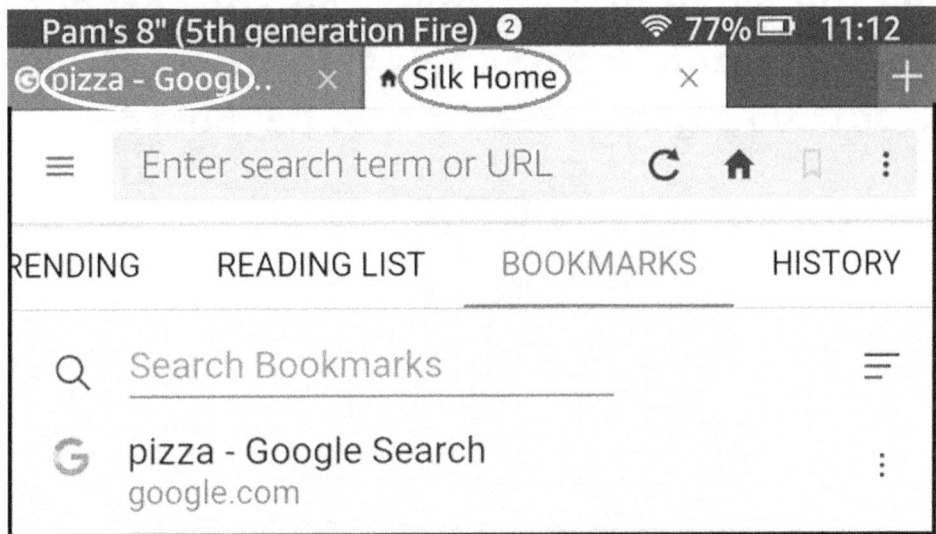

You can go to another web site using this new tab.

**Tap in the box that says "Enter search term or URL"**

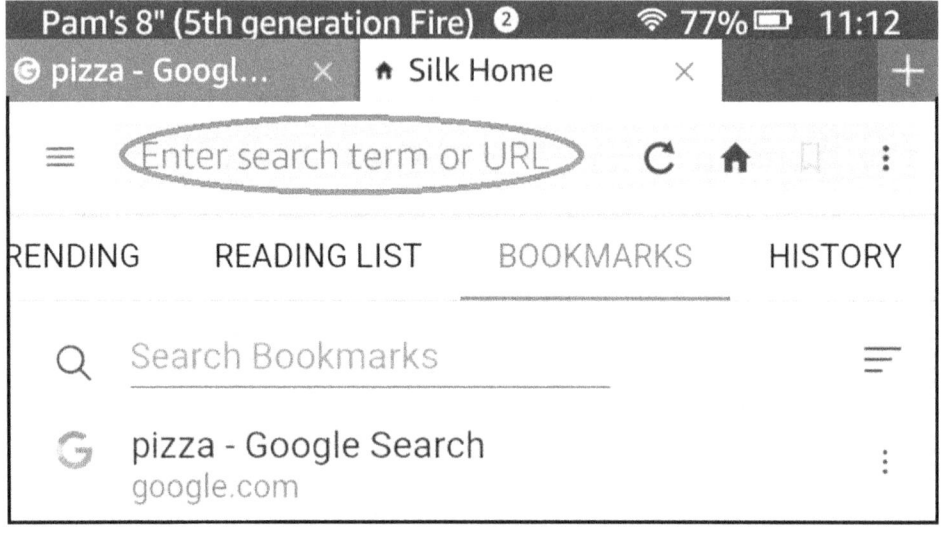

The keyboard will come up at the bottom of the screen.

**Type the name of a business, person, product into the search box and tap the yellow circle at the bottom right corner of the keyboard.**

**Only one tab on the tab bar will be white**. *(The other tabs are grey.)* **This white tab shows you the web site that is appearing on the screen.**

A tab is like a street sign.  It tells where you are <u>at the present time</u> on the screen ... the name of the web site.

You can go to many web sites, such as **<u>Sears, Ford Cars</u>, <u>JC Penney.</u>**  You can easily compare items in two stores by setting up tabs for each store, bookmarking the two tabs if you wish, and then go back and forth between the tabs comparing items.

You could type in **the name of a movie star or entertainer** and read about the person.

You can type **NFL** or **NBA** or **PGA** and get scores and information.

You can look for clothing by typing in the type of clothing, such as **women's blouses**.

Each time you go to an internet site the tab identifies the site.

*If the web-page has been **bookmarked** it will be listed with other bookmarked sites on the **Silk Home** page.*

There are so many unexpected things sold on Internet!

**Amazingly I just typed "paper clips" into a Google search and found that many listings came on screen for "paper clips" such as ...**

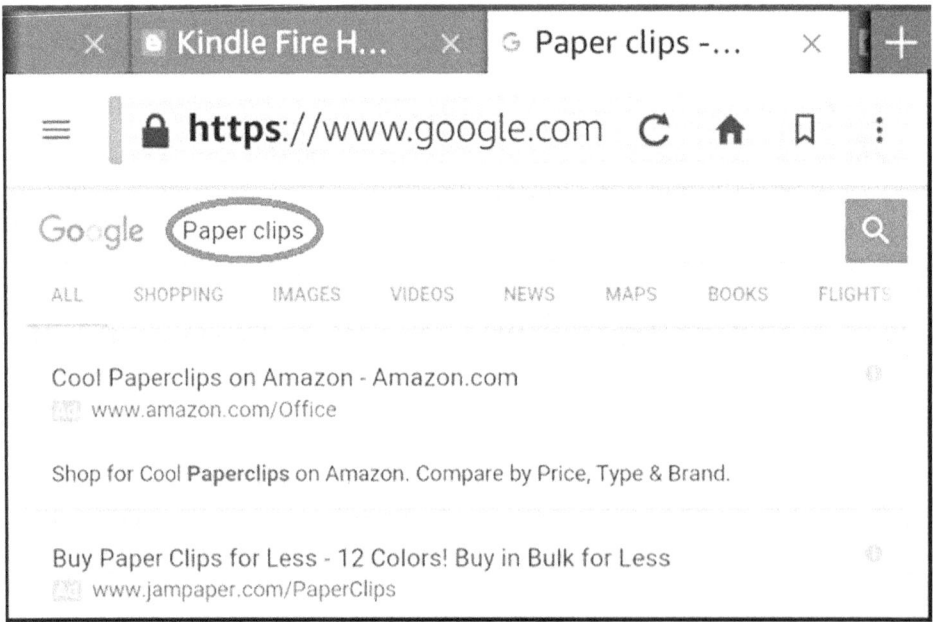

# Setting The Default Search Engine

Search engines allow you to search for items on the Internet. Two of the more popular search engines are Google and Bing. Kindle makes provision for the use of Google, Bing, or Yahoo.

If you have a preference, you can make that selection as follows:

Put your finger on the left side of the Silk Browser screen.

Drag your finger toward the middle of the screen.

A narrow screen comes on the left side of the screen ...

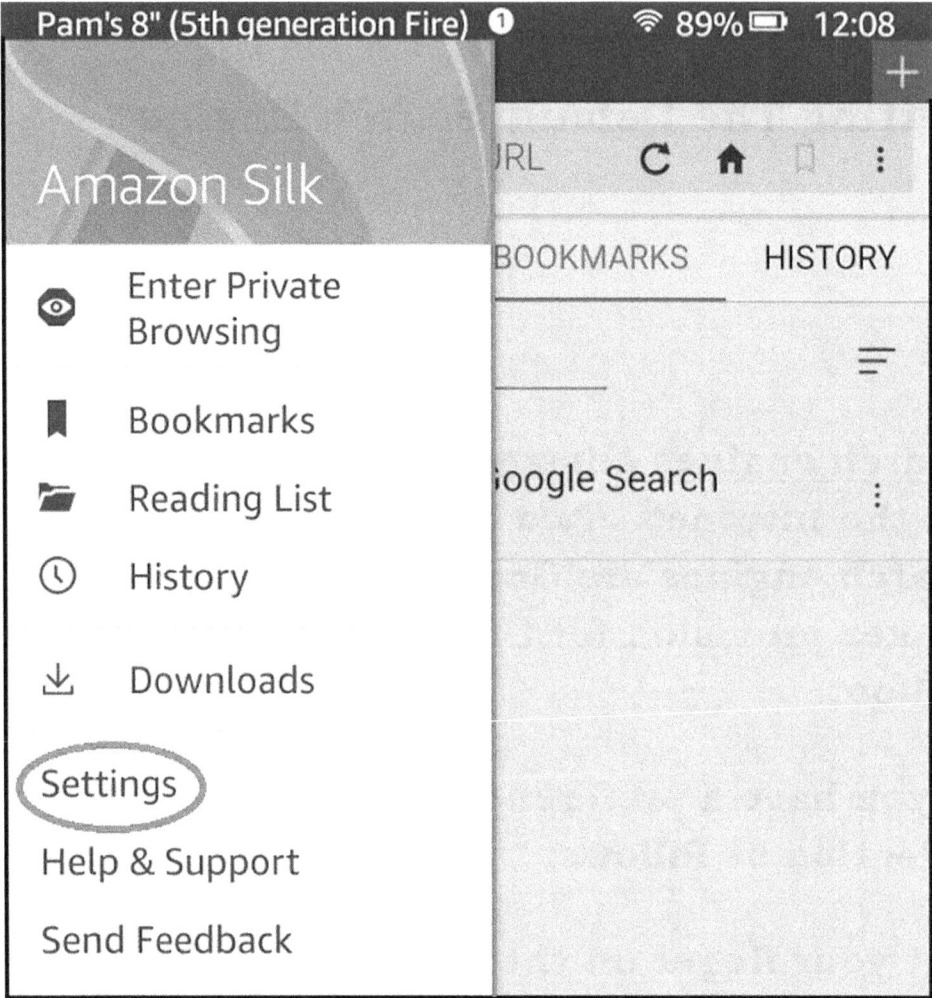

**Tap on Settings.**

Another screen comes up ...

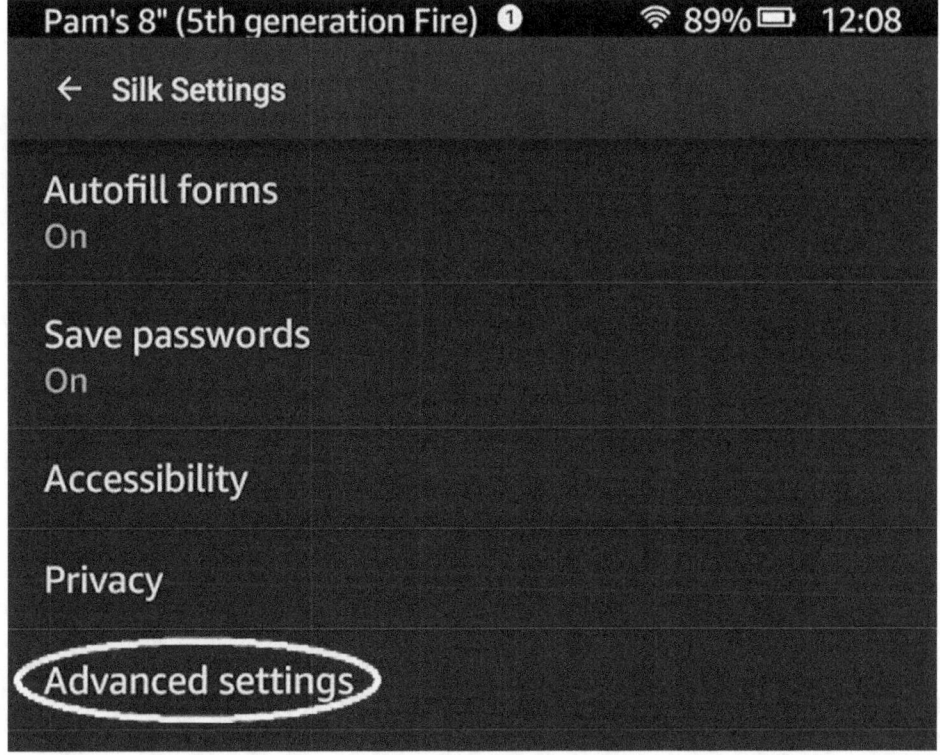

**Tap on Advanced settings**

At the top of the Advanced settings screen you'll see ...

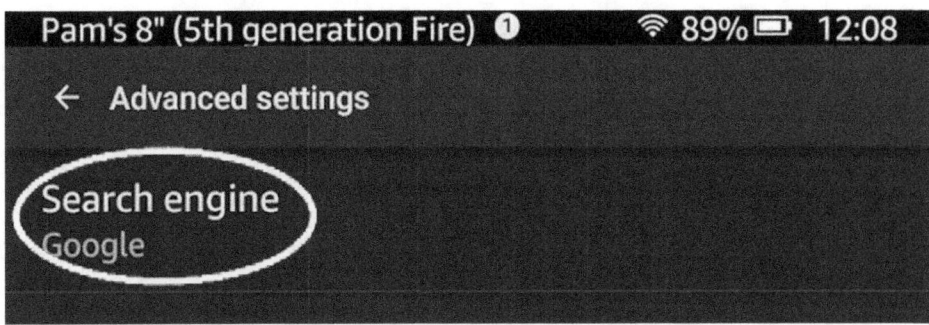

**Tap on Search engine**.

The following comes on the screen ...

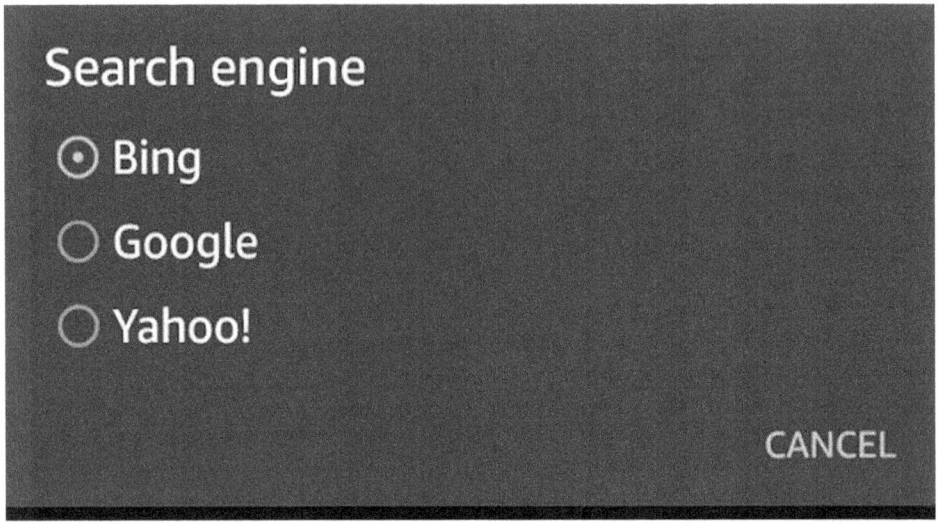

Tap on the Search engine you want to use.

After you make your selection, this screen will go away.

Tap the back arrow  at the top left corner of the screen two times to go back to the Silk Browser screen.

# Refreshing The Screen (To See Current Information)

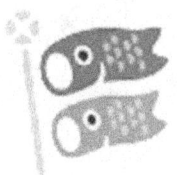

**The refresh symbol** $\circlearrowright$ lets us refresh the screen to get the most up-to-date information on the screen. This is important when using web sites that may change (update) the information shown on the screen.

**Tap the refresh symbol** $\circlearrowright$ **to refresh the screen with the most up-to-date information.**

# Removing a Tab

You can remove tabs that you no longer want to use. On the right side of each tab is an "X".

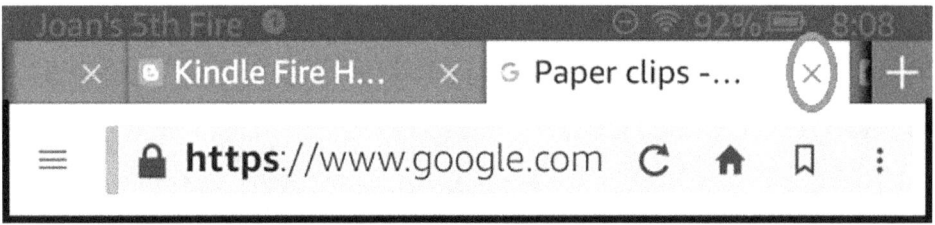

**Tap on the "X" on the right side of a tab you want to close.**

NOTE: There must always be one tab on the screen, so you can delete all but one of the tabs.

# 13. Playing Internet Radio Through Kindle

## Public Radio Stations *(free to listener)*

### Unbelievable sound reproduction ...

If I hadn't heard it, I wouldn't have believed this Kindle device could produce the sound quality it does.

**"TUNE IN RADIO"** is free and provides a wide selection of music from several PBS classical music stations ... and modern popular music stations.

## Loading The "TuneIn" App

To get **"TuneIn" radio** on your Kindle, go to Home Page ...  tap on **"Amazon store"** icon:

**Tap on the "Search"** box at top of screen. A keyboard will appear on your Kindle.

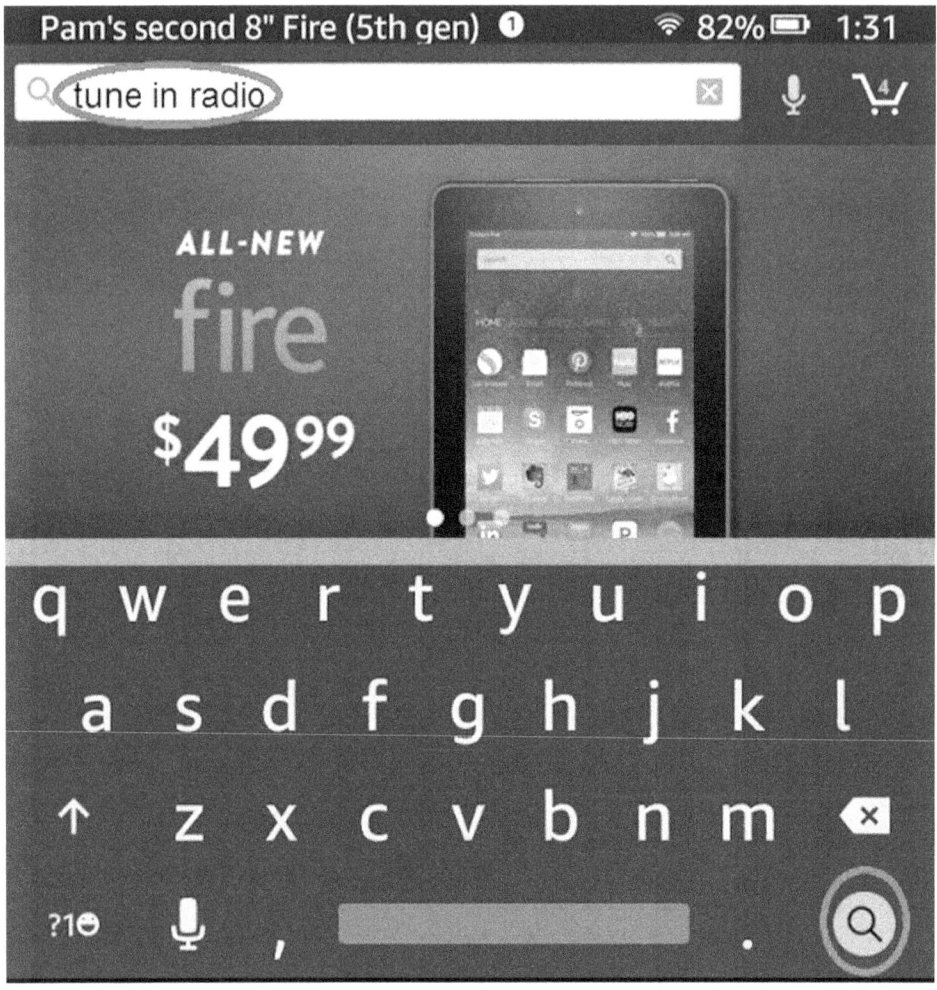

Type **"tune in radio"** in the search box.

**Tap the yellow circle on bottom right of keyboard.**

The TuneIn Radio **logo** appears …

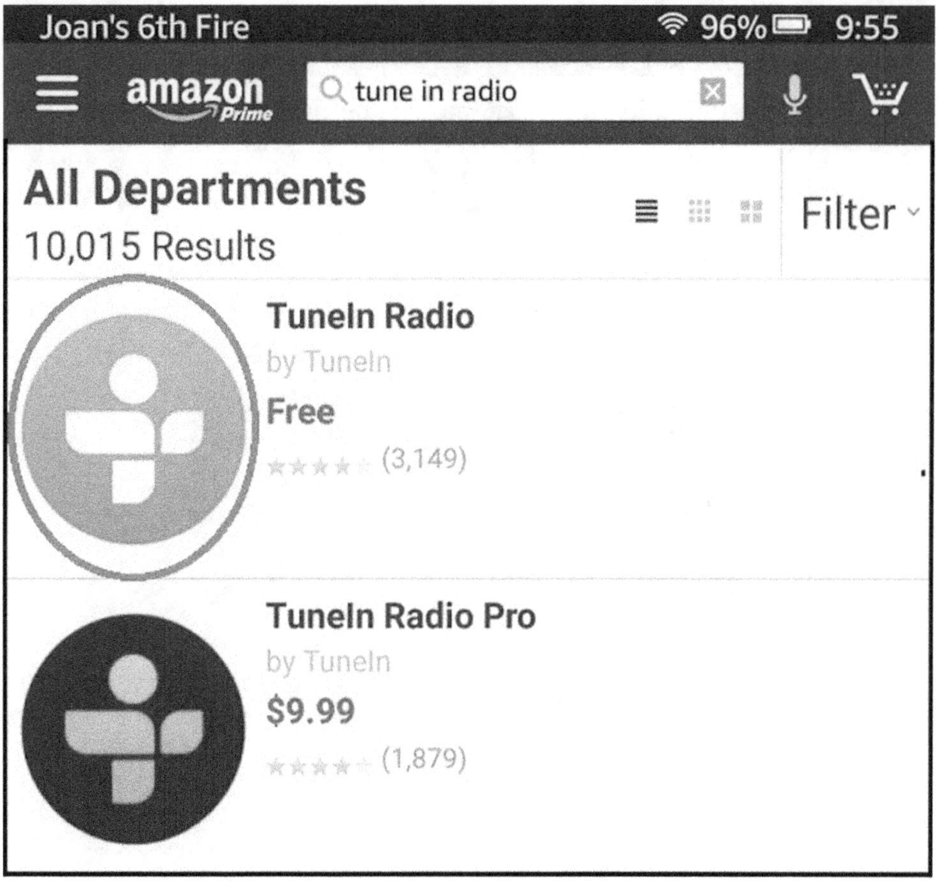

Joan's 6th Fire　　　🛜 96% 🔋 9:55

≡　amazon _Prime_　　🔍 tune in radio　　　⊠　🎤　🛒

**All Departments**
10,015 Results　　　　　　≡ ⋮⋮ ⋮⋮ | Filter ˅

**TuneIn Radio**
by TuneIn
**Free**
★★★★☆ (3,149)

**TuneIn Radio Pro**
by TuneIn
**$9.99**
★★★★☆ (1,879)

It is **free** app.

**Tap on the logo for TuneIn Radio.**

Scroll down on screen until you see **"Buy from Amazon Store"** in a yellow box.

**Tap on this yellow box**. (It is free ... $0.00 will be on this screen)

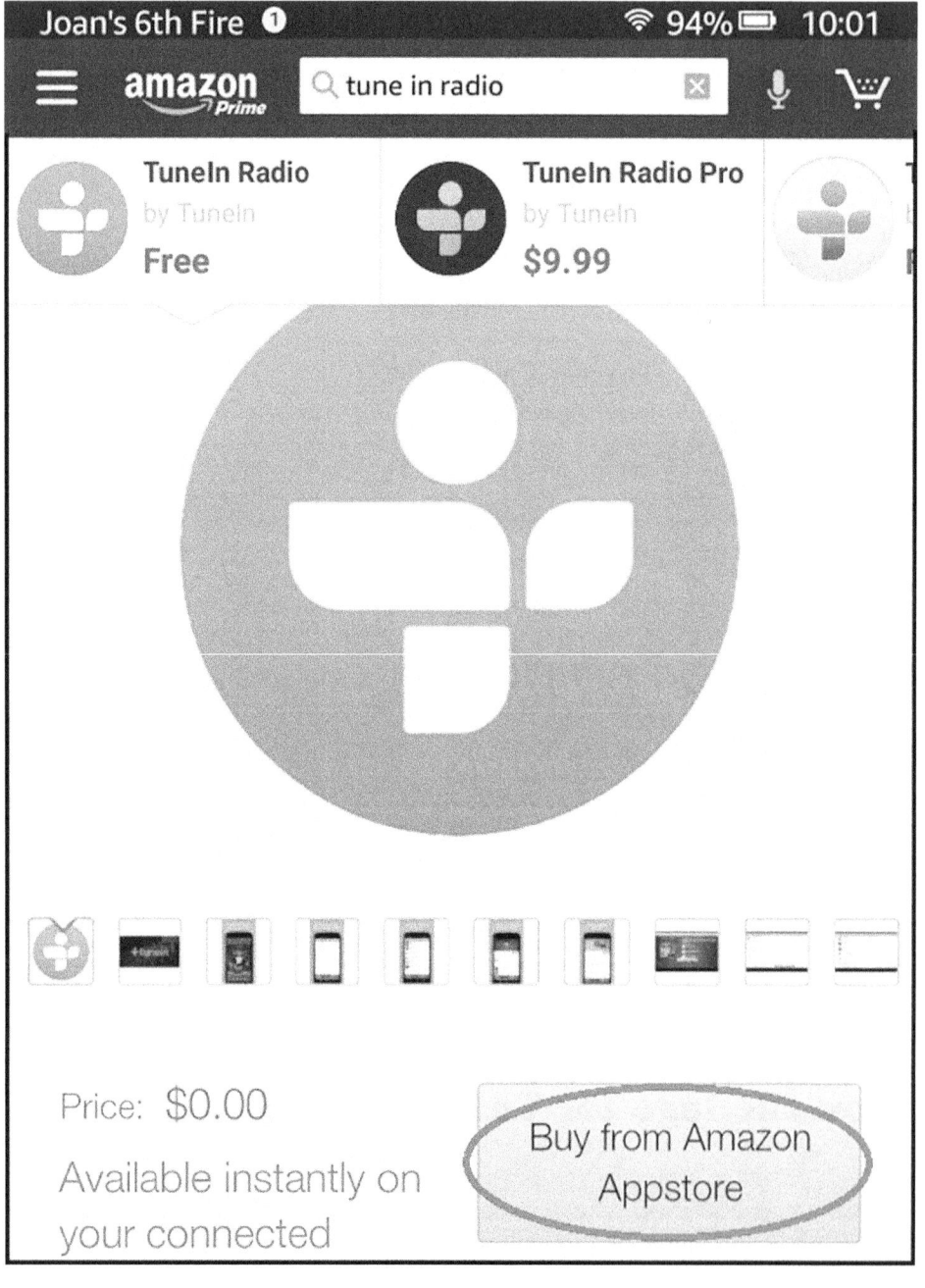

Another screen will come up with a box which says **"Download"**.

**Tap on the Download box**.  The TuneIn app will download and be installed on your Kindle.

When TuneIn has downloaded and been installed on your Kindle, you will then see a yellow box on screen that says "**OPEN**".

**Tap on OPEN** and TuneIn will open on screen.

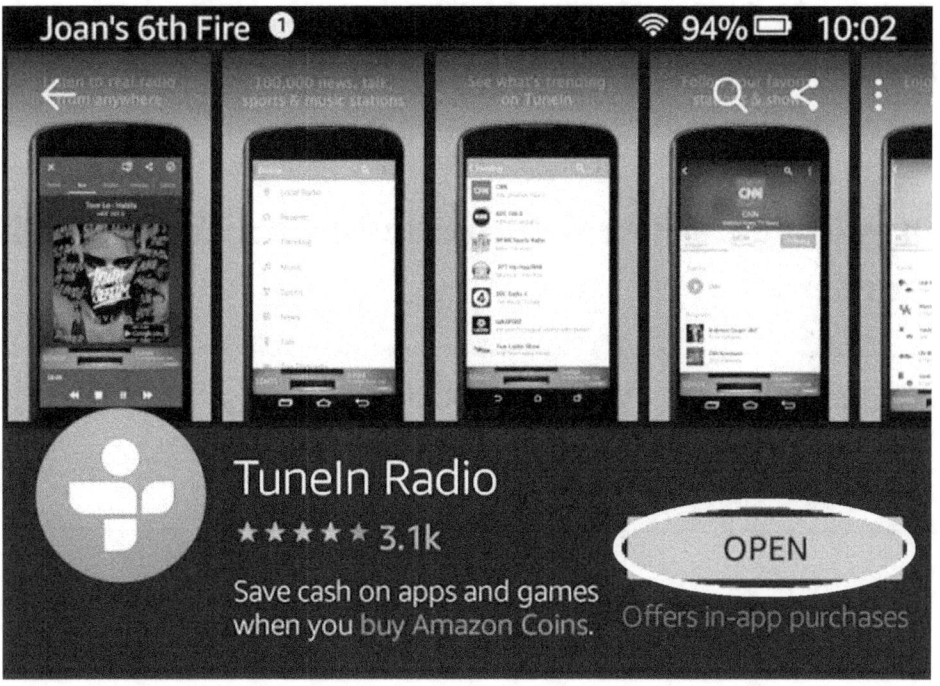

The **"TuneIn" logo** will also appear on your home page.

After the app downloads onto your Kindle, you will find an icon has been automatically added onto the list of icons on your Kindle Home Page ...

...**scroll** to the bottom of the Home Page by holding your finger on the Kindle Home page screen and moving finger toward top of screen.

**You will see several more icons on "lower half" of screen.**

The last icon added, **"TuneIn Radio",** will appear in the icon list.

# Bringing In Music After App Is Installed

Go to **Home Page** ...tap on the **TuneIn icon**

The radio station categories will appear.

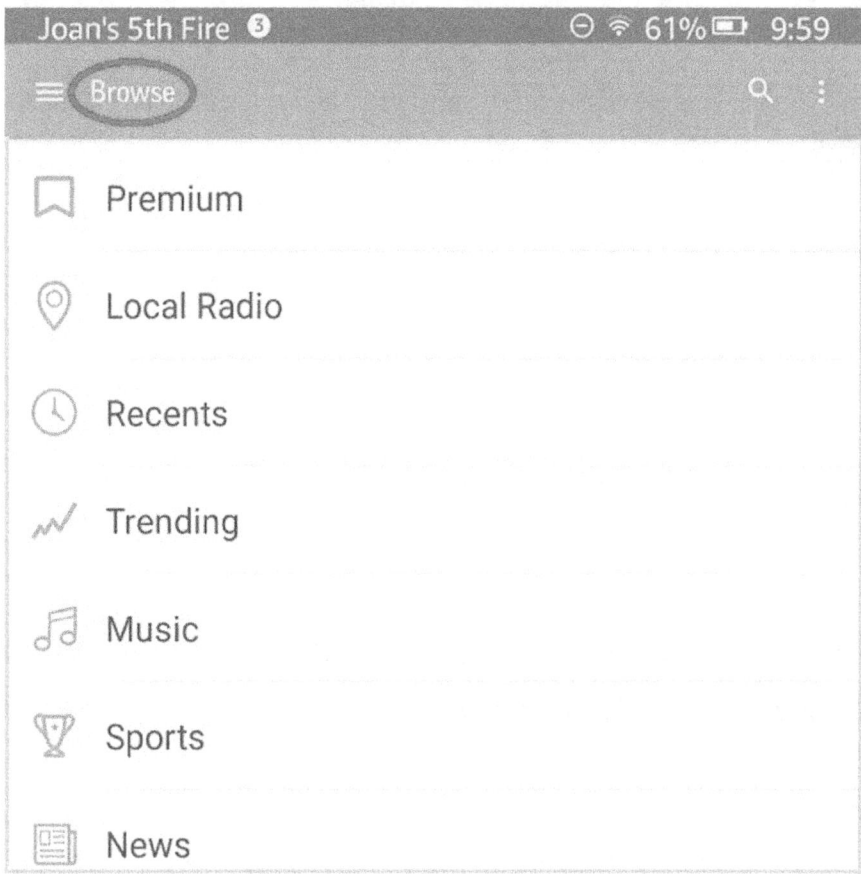

## Browse screen:  Music

Tap on MUSIC and several categories of music will appear, including ...

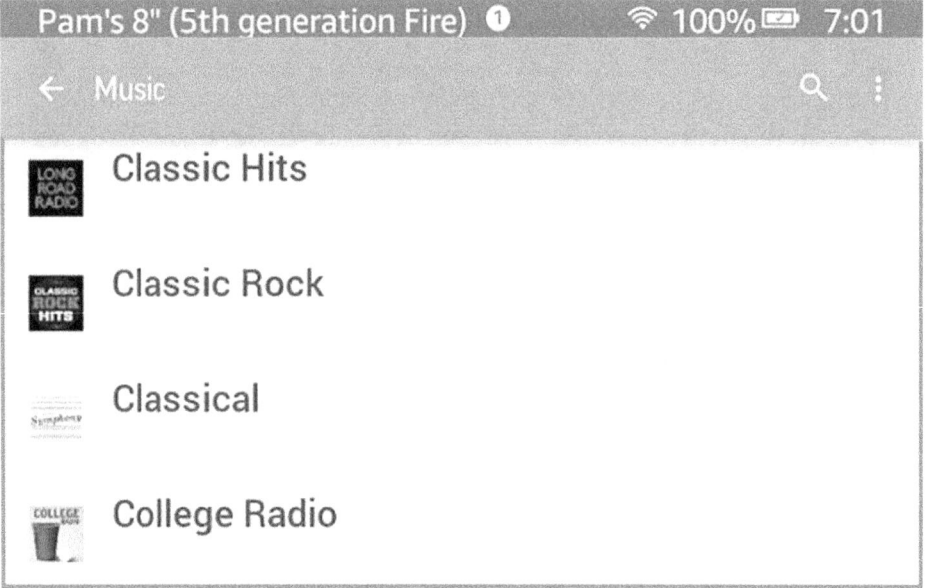

**Tap on a type of music:  classical or country western or rock or 60's**

Several stations will appear in a list.

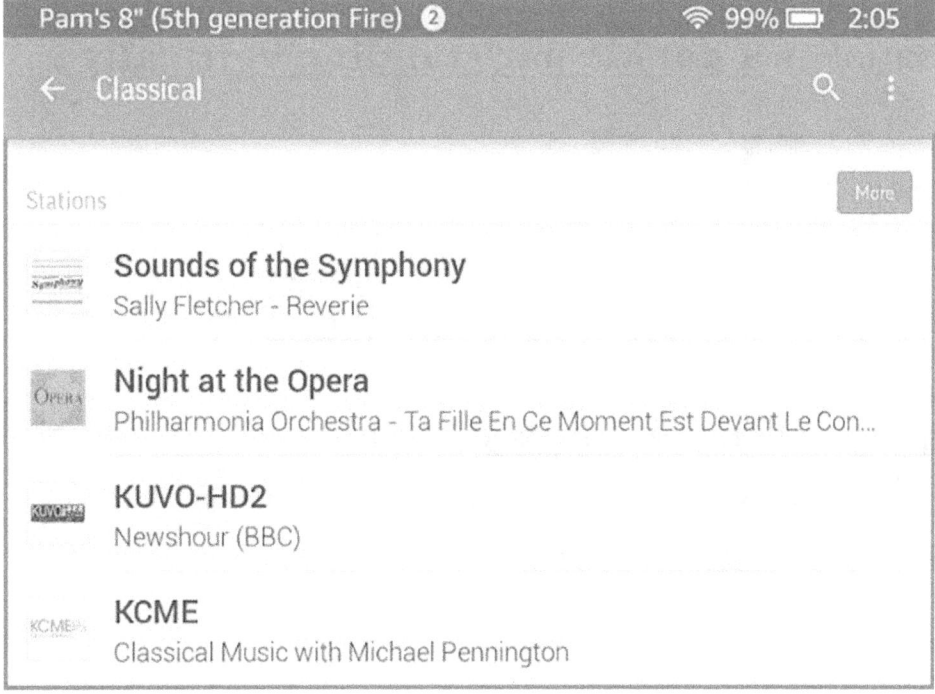

Tap on the logo of the station of your choice.

On the next screen, tap on the green circle next to the station you have chosen.

A screen for that station will come up and music will begin playing **in a few seconds.**

You might also need to tap on **the forward sign** which is like **an arrow** pointing toward the right .

play ...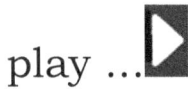

...pause is **a double bar standing vertically** ...

pause ...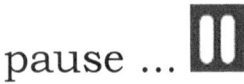

...stop is **a square box. stop** ....

Tap on the arrow **to play** the music.  Tap on the double bar **to pause** the music.  Tap on the square box **to turn off** the radio.

***The sound of the Kindle is amazingly high quality for such a small size device.***  *I was really surprised in the quality of sound and now I listen to radio often through the Kindle.  For me this is an added bonus to owning the Kindle.  (I am having a little volume problem with **TuneIn** ... I also have subscription to **Amazon Prime**.  It is even better sound quality than **TuneIn** and there is no volume problem.)*

# 14. Amazon Prime: Music, Video, Books

## Introduction To Amazon Prime

Three icons on your Home Page can be used to access music, videos, and books you have purchased or uploaded as well as which are available through Amazon Prime.

**Amazon Prime** is one of the subscription offerings on Kindle. The membership is approximately $99.00 per year. *(Amazon Prime offers a free trial for one month.)*

In **<u>MUSIC</u>, the sound quality is very good.**

Even if you have not subscribed to Amazon Prime, you will still be able to receive and play music which you have purchased from Amazon.

Tap once on the **Amazon Music icon** on home page. When you do this one of three categories will come on your Kindle screen: Recent Activity, Prime Music, or Library. **You need to be on the Recent Activity page. Check upper left corner of screen to see which page is currently appearing on your screen. 4-items are listed under "Recent Activities" as follows: PLAYED ADDED DOWNLOADED PURCHASED**.

**Tap on "PURCHASED" to see the items you have bought from Amazon music.**

**With Amazon Prime**, you receive streaming movies and TV episodes, books to borrow for free *(limited to 2 per month)*, and an excellent catalog of music for streaming.

For approximately $10 monthly fee (added to the basic subscription fee), you can join **Kindle Unlimited** which gives you access to books designated as **Kindle Unlimited** when you order books. You are permitted to have up to 10 books checked out at a time. There is no charge for books at Amazon when they are marked "**Kindle**

**<u>Unlimited</u>**" and you can download these and use them "on loan" as you would do at a library. This way you have access to more than 2 "free" books per month if you are avid reader.

*(Also with Amazon Prime, people receive free two day shipping <u>when shopping with Amazon </u>when product is eligible for Prime shipping. Amazon states that most products that are offered on Amazon and are fulfilled by Amazon warehouses will be eligible for free two day shipping. Within certain cities you can get free same day delivery. Limitations apply and must be checked at time of order.)*

**Due to extensive offerings provided in the area of Amazon music, the next 3 chapters are devoted to instructions.**

# 15. Music: Categories

**Amazon Music** lets you play music from Your Music Library.  Your Music Library may contain music selections you have purchased or uploaded, or which are available through your Amazon Prime subscription.

**Tap on the following icon on Home Page to get to Amazon Music.**

## Recent Activities, Prime Music, Library

Amazon divided their Music Screen into 3 major categories:  (with sub-categories under each major category)

| Recent Activities | Prime Music | Library |
|---|---|---|
| - Played | - Stations | - Playlists |
| - Added | - Playlists | - Albums |
| - Downloaded | - Songs | - Artists |
| - Purchased | - Albums | - Songs |
| | | - Genres |

When you **tap on the icon for Amazon Music** *(located on your home screen)* as follows:

... one of the 3 major categories of music will appear on your screen.

**Recent Activity**
**Prime Music**
**Library (Cloud Library)**

**Look on the upper left side** *(of your screen)* **and you will see one of the above categories.**

In the following example, you will see the "**Recent Activity**" screen.

At the top left side notice the title of the screen: **"Recent Activity"**

**Learn to check the screen title.** Then you will know where you are.

- **Recent Activity**
- **Prime Music**
- **Library**

**Under "Recent Activity" there are 4 subjects:**

**PLAYED   ADDED   DOWNLOADED   PURCHASED**

**One will be underlined.** This is what you are seeing on your screen at the current time.

**On screen**, there will be lists of music for you to choose from or there will be album jackets to choose. **If you tap on one of these**, that jacket will appear on screen and music will begin playing.

**(Turn the volume up or down by pressing on one of the silver bars at the top edge of your Kindle. The bar on the left lowers the volume. The bar on the right raises the volume.)**

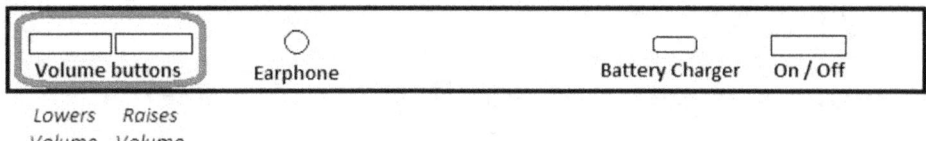

Volume buttons          Earphone               Battery Charger    On / Off

*Lowers   Raises*
*Volume   Volume*

# Finding Main Menu

**To locate menu:**  **Put your finger down on left side of screen.  Hold finger down and drag finger toward center of screen.  A menu will come up as follows:**

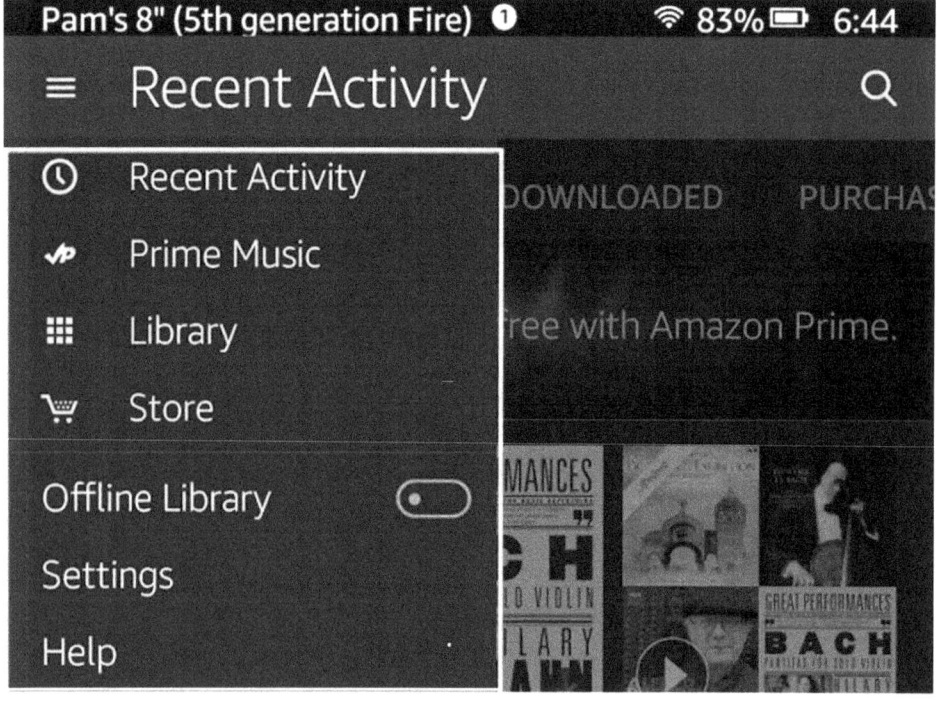

**You can tap on each listing in this menu to bring up specific categories:** _Recent Activities_, _Prime Music_, _Library_, _Store_, _Offline Library_, _Settings_, _Help_

**To remove menu:**  Place finger on center of screen and drag finger (swipe) to left.

# To Get From Music Screen Back To Main Menu

**At top side of screen, beside the name of the category that is currently on screen, you will see 3 lines stacked.**

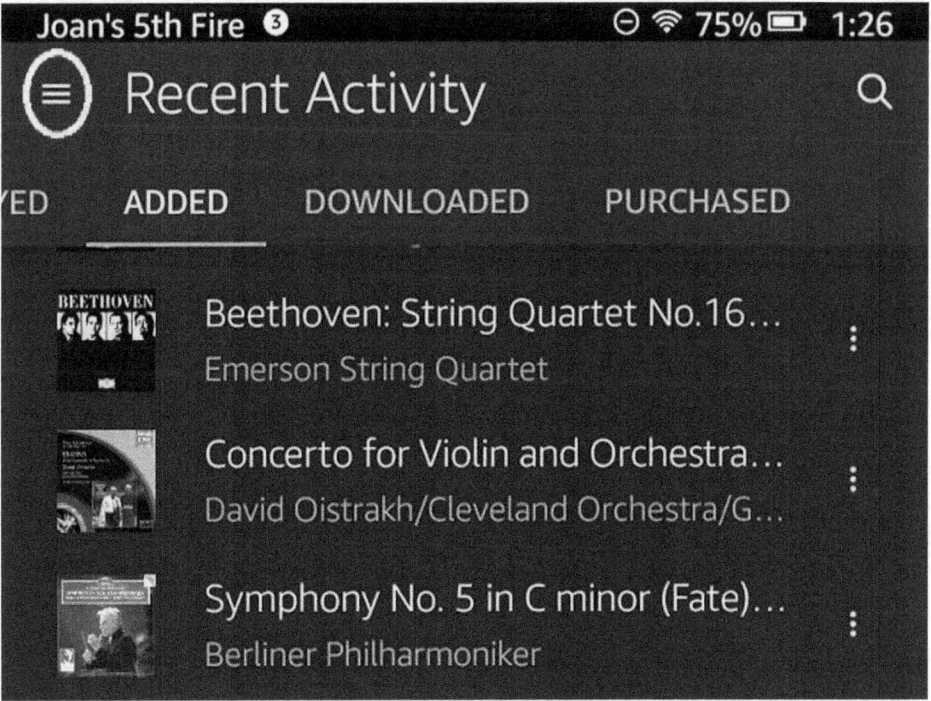

Tap that symbol of the 3 lines stacked ... This will take you back to the **Main Menu** ... *(if there is an arrow at the top instead of the 3 lines stacked, tap that arrow. Another screen will appear that does have the 3 lines stacked in upper left corner. Now tap the 3 lines stacked to get back to main menu.)*

Now you are back at **Main Menu** ...

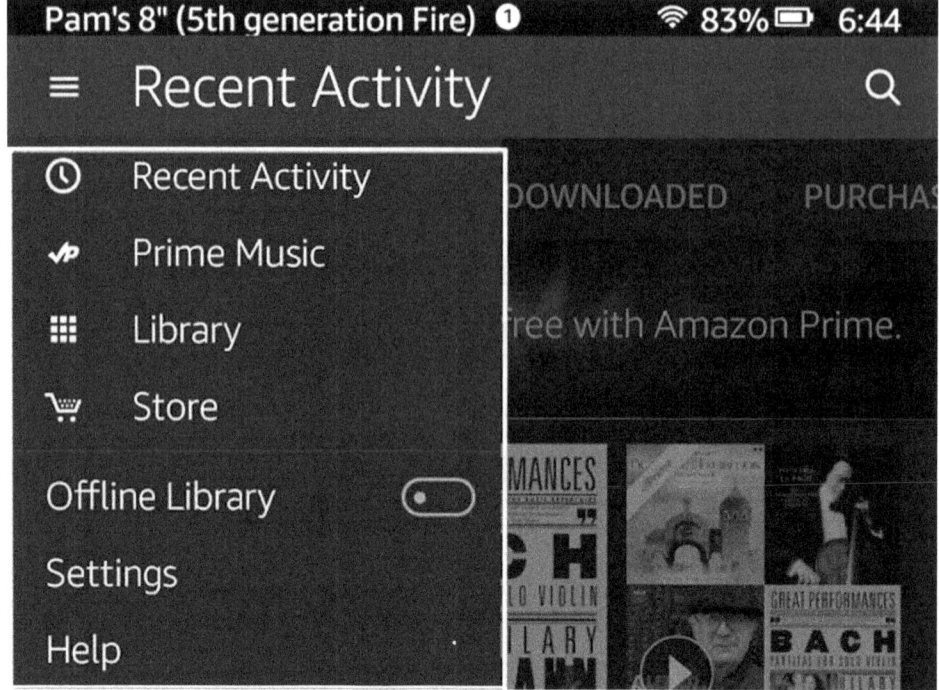

**There are 2 ways to get back to Main Menu:**

**- finger pressed on left side of screen / drag finger to center of screen**

**- tap on the 3 lines at top left side of screen**

**The next chapter, Music: Compositions contains more about finding various compositions, songs, artists, albums.**

# 16. Music: Compositions

**You will need a high speed Wi-Fi to stream music.**

Most will have such in using Kindle. If you are in hospital or nursing home, these might be available to you. Ask the nurse.

At home, many will now have these through their Wi-Fi.

If you are using your Kindle music **away from home,** you will likely need to have some music downloaded onto your Kindle.

## Downloading Music

**This is easy to do on your Kindle.**

**From your Home Page, tap Amazon Music icon.**

**Beside the composition (song) that comes onscreen, you will see 3 dots lined up vertically.** *(Sometimes on albums these three dots appear below the album on right corner of album.)*

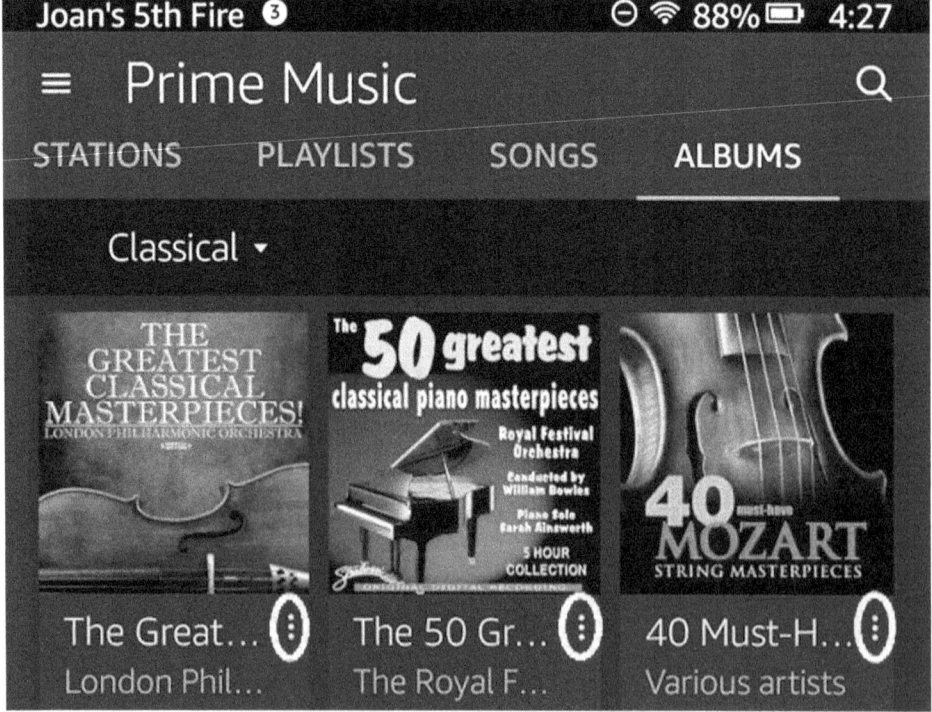

**Tap on the 3 dots.**

Another menu comes on screen with several

**Tap the "download"** option and the music will download onto your Kindle.


**Give time for music to download:** *Usually a symbol will appear on screen in form of a circle and you will see yellow line moving around the circle showing activity is taking place. This composition is downloading.*

*When the circle is completely surrounded it will disappear. The downloading is complete.*

# To Locate Downloaded Music

## On main menu:  Click on "Recent Activity" ...

(**Remember** "**main menu**".  You get to it by holding down finger on left side of screen and dragging finger toward center of screen.  The main menu appears on left side of screen.  Or you can return to main menu by one tap on the 3 stacked lines at top left corner of the screen.)

Now tap on "Recent Activity" on main menu...

## Under "Recent Activity", you will see 4 options:  PLAYED, ADDED, DOWNLOADED, PURCHASED.

Tap "**DOWNLAODED**".  The music you have downloaded will be listed on the screen.

It is now ready for you to play when you leave your home and do not have Wi-Fi connection.

# Excellence Of Classical Music Selections

**In classical music, the quality of performers, conductors, orchestras is incredible.** To name a few:  conductors, George Szell / Sir Thomas Schippers / Bruno Walter ... cellists, Jacqueline du Pre  / Lynn Harrell / Yo Yo Ma / and the great cellist and teacher, Leonard Rose ... violinists Itzhak Perlman / David Oistrakh /Zino Francescatti / Henryk Szeryng / the entire recordings of the Bach unaccompanied violin sonatas and partitas *(these are just some of the compositions and artists <u>available</u>)*

**<u>About the sound quality:</u>** Extremely pure sound, devoid of extraneous noise. **<u>In Classical music</u>** you want a sound which is as close as possible in texture to the individual musical instrument. This is amazingly pure sound for the instruments for such a small device.

**In the next chapter, <u>Music: Locations</u> we discuss locating specific sets of music on your Kindle.**

# 17. Music: Locations

## Recent Activities Category

This will bring to screen those compositions and artists which you have **recently** played on Kindle.

**If you look at the screen of "Recent Activity", you will see sub-topics:**

   **PLAYED   ADDED   DOWNLOADED   PURCHASED**

(One of the above will be **underlined** on your screen.  This will tell you the screen that you are currently seeing on your Kindle.)

**If you tap on "PLAYED" you will see screen of albums you have recently played.**

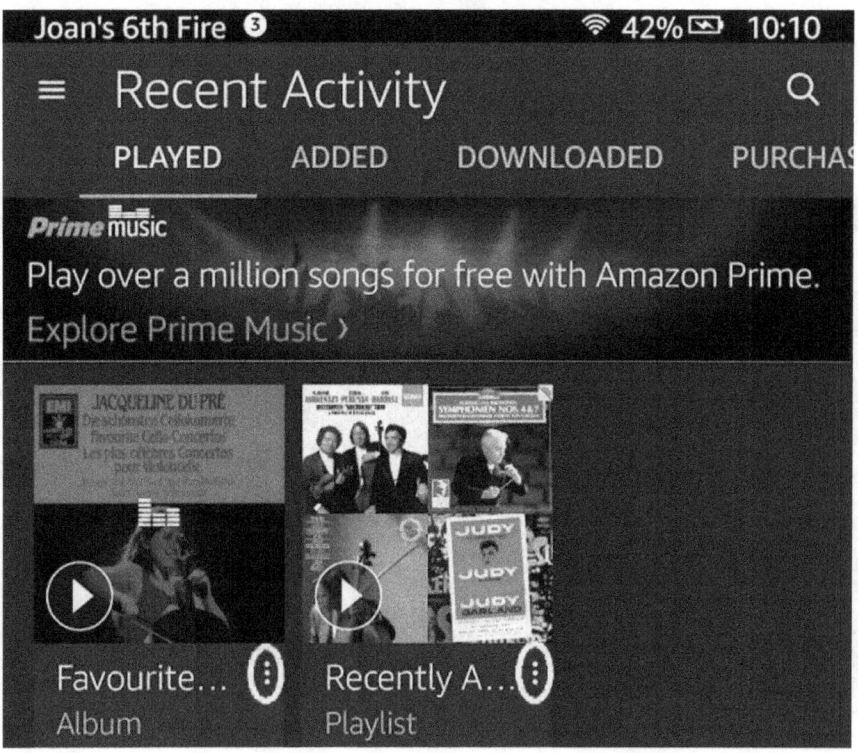

At the bottom of the album, you will see **three**

**dots standing in a row.**

Anytime you see this on Kindle, if you tap on these three dots, a smaller menu will come up on screen, such as the following, **giving you choices.**

Go to Playlist

Download

Remove From Recently Played

Now tap on "**ADDED**" under the "Recent Activity" page.  The <u>added screen</u> will appear.

**NOTICE THOSE 3 DOTS** at the side of each composition.

**Remember: 3 dots means a small menu is there giving you choices about that composition.**

Tap on the 3 dots at the side of one of the compositions in the list. A small menu will appear such as follows:

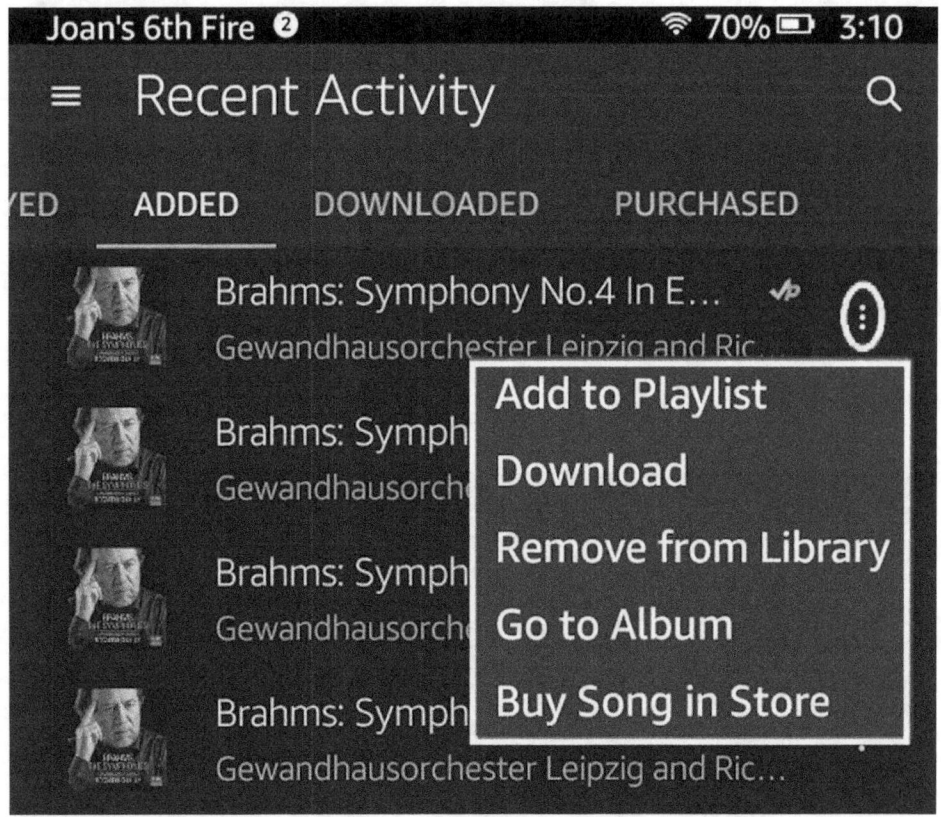

**Recent Activity** page ... the next item under "recent activity" is **DOWNLOADED** ... **Tap on "DOWNLOADED".** This will bring up all the

compositions you have downloaded. A screen shows your downloaded compositions.
*(Remember: these downloaded items can be played on Kindle even when you are away from a Wi-Fi connection ... that is to say away from your home.)*

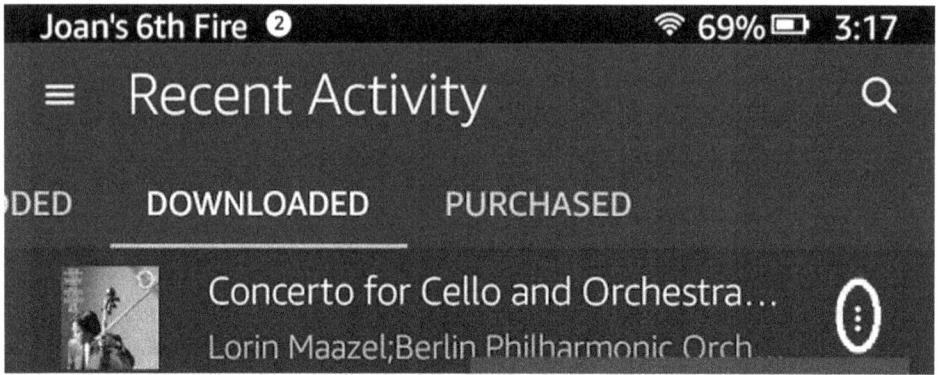

**Do you notice the 3 little dots at the end of the line of each composition?** Remember: This means a menu is available, giving you choices for this composition.

**Tap on the 3 dots**. A menu screen will come up.

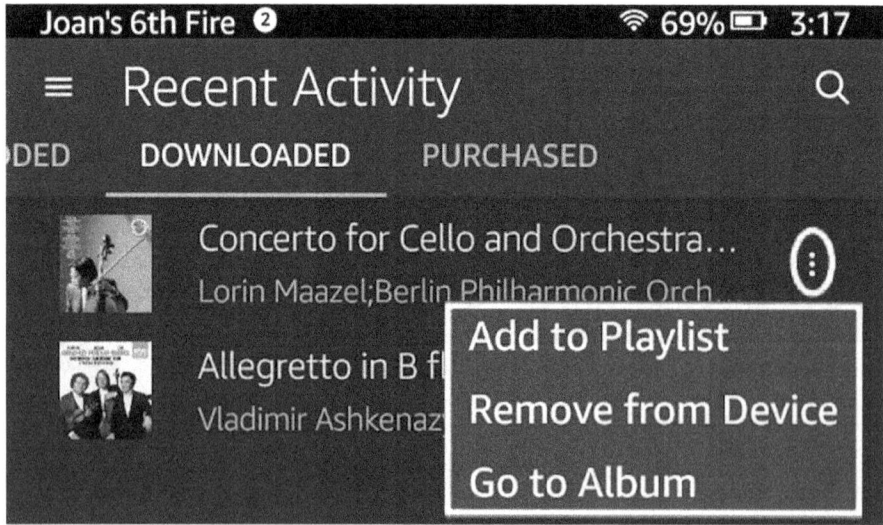

The 4th category under "Recent Activity" is **"PURCHASED"** .  Here you see music you have purchased from Amazon.

You can purchase music from Amazon by going to the Store on the main menu ... You do not have to be member of Amazon Prime to receive and to hear on Kindle the music purchased from Amazon.

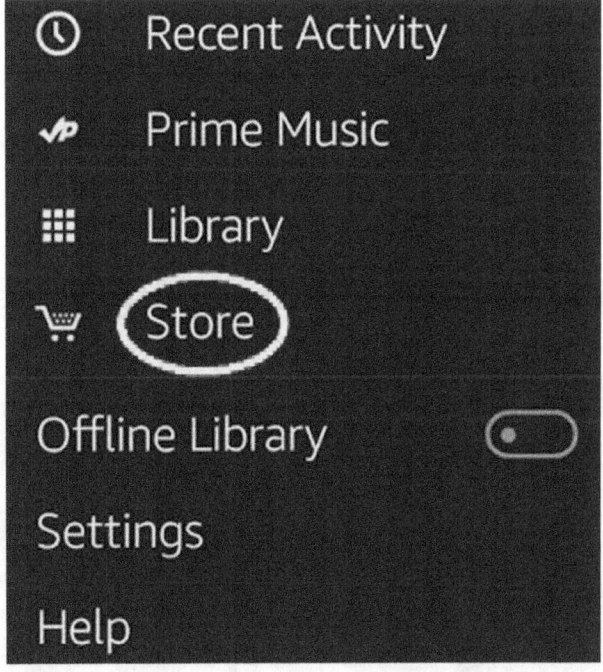

Use the Search to find a specific song, artist, or album.  Tap on the magnifying glass in the top

right corner of the screen.

To place your order, tap the button displaying the price.  Tap **Buy** (for songs) or **Buy Album** (for albums) to confirm your purchase.

# Prime Music Category

**To get to "<u>Prime Music</u>"** from "Recent Activity", tap on the 3 parallel lines on the top left side of the page. ▤ *(or you can press finger on left side of screen and drag finger to center of screen)* This will bring "Main Menu" up on left side of your screen.

<u>**Look closely at this list from main menu.**</u>

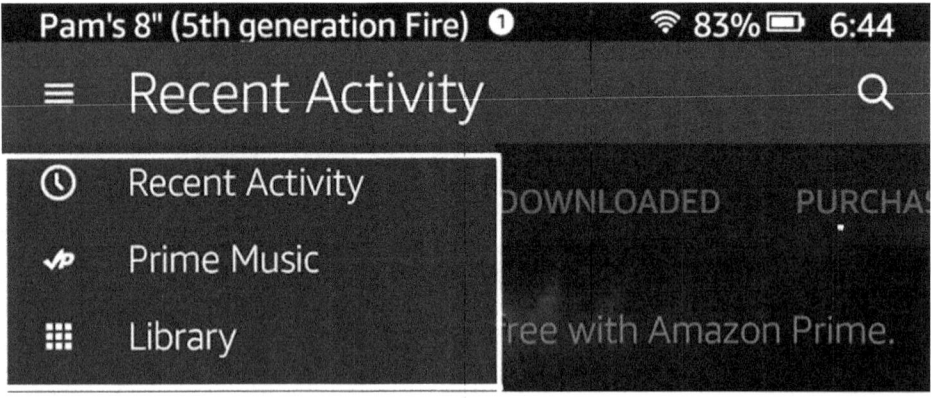

**Notice the listings starting with the<u> clock symbol</u> ... which shows "Recent Activities" ...**

**Then there is <u>another symbol</u> ... which is "Prime Music"...**

**Another symbol** *(3 rows of dots stacked on one another)* **is "Library" (Cloud Library)** ...

<u>**These are the main areas where you will find music located**</u> ... **these 3 areas.**

**Then under each of these 3 areas, you will find 4 sub-topics which have music listings.** *(an extra sub-topic will appear on a "carousel" in the Cloud Library area)*

<u>**If you can begin thinking this way, you will be able to navigate through the Amazon Music section.**</u>

**3 main areas:  Recent Activity / Prime Music / Cloud Library**

**4 sub-topics under each main area.**

<u>**This is where all the music is located.**</u>

## From the Main Menu: Tap on "Prime Music" .

...The Prime Music screen will appear on your device.  <u>You must have a current subscription with Amazon Prime to see music in this area</u>.

Look at the sub-headings:  (viewed in the following)

**Notice one of these 4 is underlined.  In the above picture,  <u>ALBUMS</u>  is** UNDERLINED.

This picture tells you that on screen, you are seeing the categories of **<u>"Prime Music"</u>** ... **<u>"ALBUMS"</u>**.

Stay in **"Prime Music"** and tap on **"STATIONS"** ... This will bring up another list of music.

Then tap on **"PLAYLISTS"**, more listings of music appears for you to choose from.

Tap **"SONGS"** ... another list appears on screen.

Tap **"ALBUMS"** ... another list of music.

**For each category there are many selections of music available.**

**While still in Prime Music ... "ALBUMS"**

Look at the following on screen ...

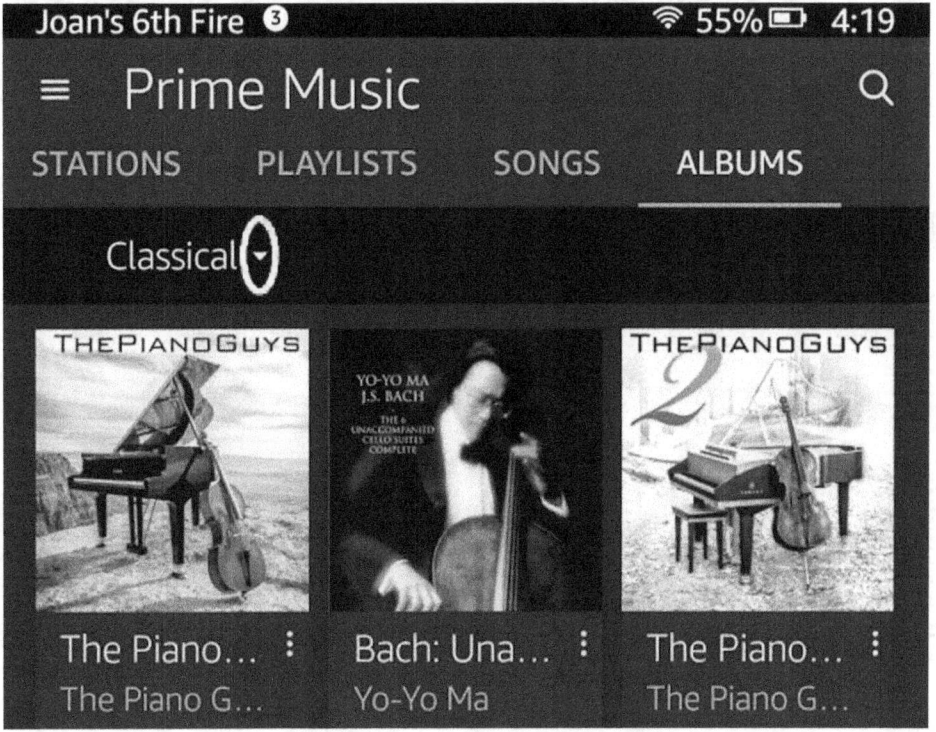

Directly under the name of "station", you will see a downward arrow.  Tap that arrow.  It will bring up a menu giving you a choice of categories such as:

Select category by tap of finger on choice of music.   Now you can begin music by one tap on the album of your choice.

## Library (Cloud Library) Category

Return to **Main Menu** , and tap on "**Library**".

This brings up a screen of "**Cloud Library**".

Cloud is a computer storage system. It is sort of like a closet where you store things not currently needed. But after it has been in storage, you can go to your closet and take out something and use it.

You have all the music available that is stored in **"Cloud Library"**.

Notice the sub-listings lined up on screen under **"Cloud Library"**.

**PLAYLISTS  ALBUMS  ARTISTS  SONGS  GENRES**

## To Create A Playlist

Take special notice of **"PLAYLIST"** in Cloud **Library ...**

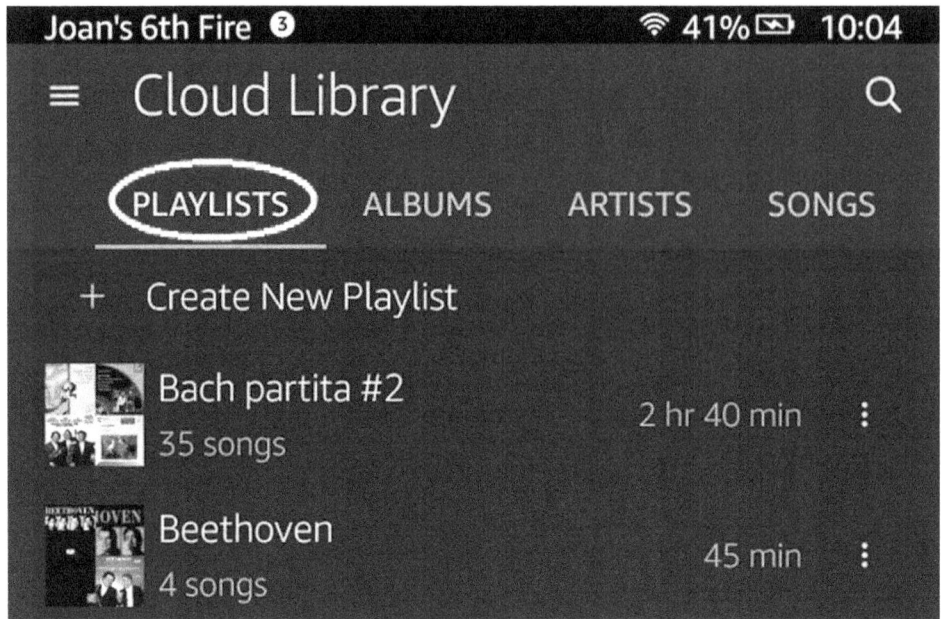

Along the way, you can **"create"** your own playlists, even giving the list the names you select.

For example:  in my **PLAYLIST** , **a few of the names I have used are:**

**Bach Concertos / Perlman**
**Bach Concertos / Hillery Hann**
**Dvorak /Jacqueline Du Pre**
**Judy Garland**
**Mozart Symphonies**

These categories mean something to me.  I can immediately locate compositions performed by various violinists, cellists, singers ...  and I can locate composers such as Bach & Mozart and some of my favorite recordings.

**The only place these personally created <u>PLAYLISTS</u> are located is in "<u>Cloud Library</u>".**

So to find the playlists I have created, I must remember to go first to the main menu and tap on **<u>Cloud Library</u>** and then tap on **<u>PLAYLIST</u>** .

To **"<u>Create a Playlist</u>" Have the music playing... then ...**

**Bring up "<u>Cloud Library</u>" and tap on <u>PLAYLIST</u>. A colored line will appear under the name "<u>PLAYLIST</u>" after you tap on PLAYLIST.**

**Under PLAYLIST you will see "<u>Create a PLAYLIST</u>".**

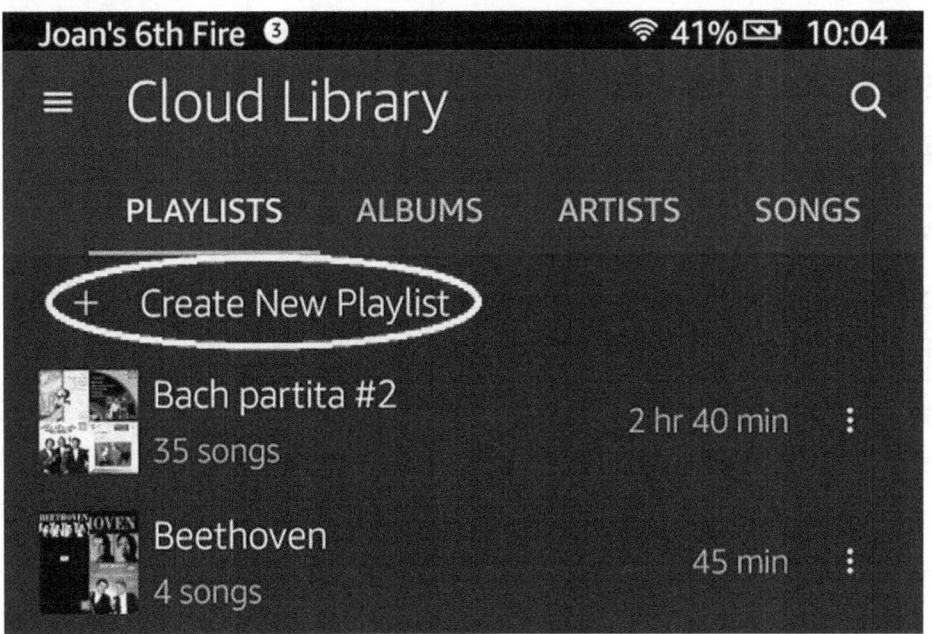

**Tap on "<u>CREATE A PLAYLIST</u>"**

When the screen comes up you can type in the name of your new playlist: *(example: Dvorak / du Pre ... telling you composer and performer which allows you to easily locate the disc)*

**Type in name and <u>tap save</u> at the bottom of the screen.**

**<u>The music you want to put on playlist should be playing as you perform this next step.</u>**

**With the music playing, tap on the 3 dots to left of the music you want to add to playlist. This will bring up a menu with the first item the name of your new playlist.**

**Tap on the name of your playlist and composition will be added to your list under that name you have chosen.**

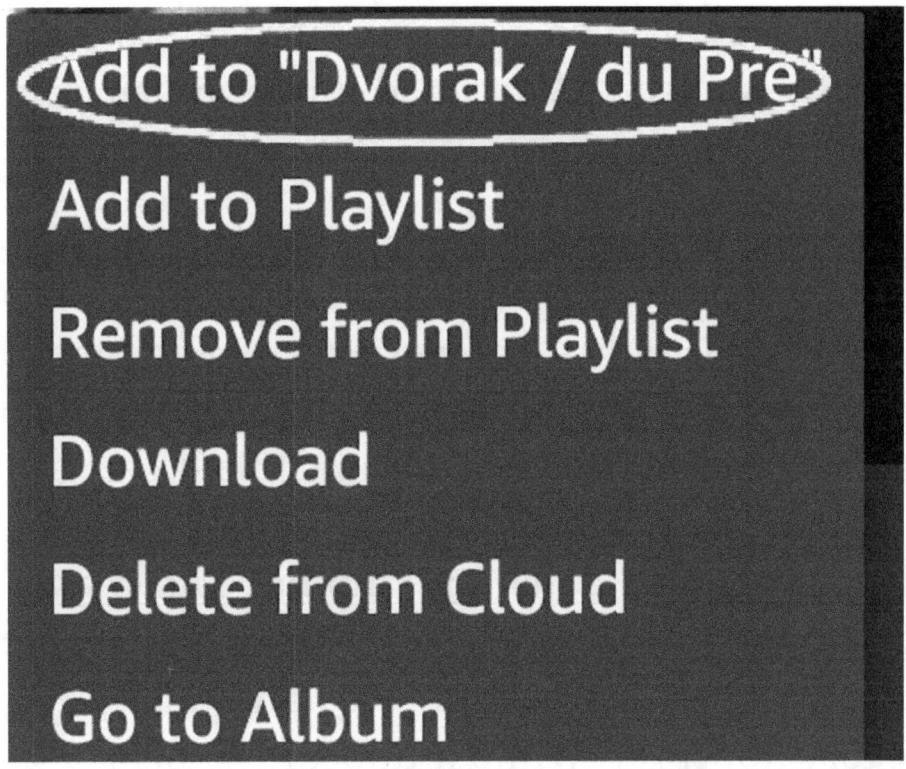

Check your **PLAYLIST**. The new title and the composer/performer should appear in the list along with the movements of the composition.

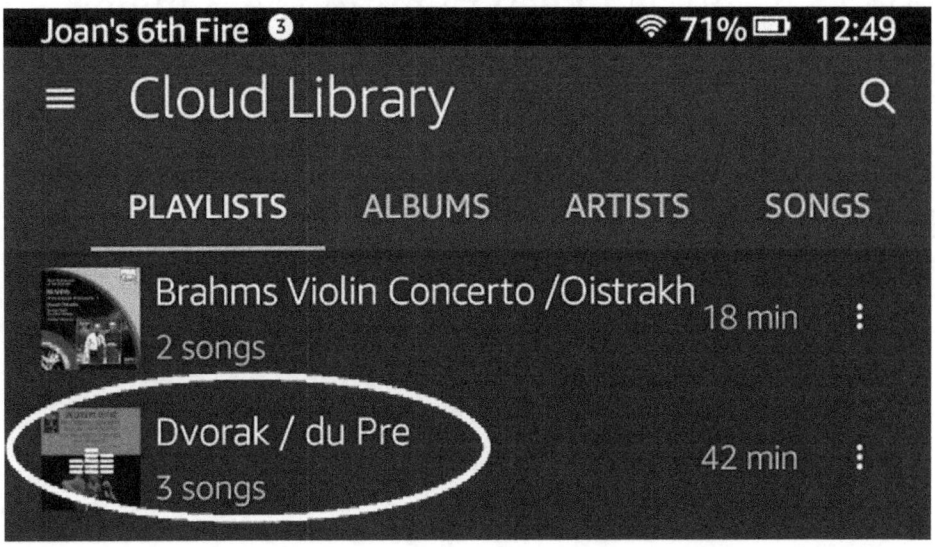

"**Cloud Library**" also contains many albums stored by Amazon.  Vast amounts of music is located in Cloud Library under the 5 categories:

**PLAYLISTS   ALBUMS   ARTISTS   SONGS   GENRES**

You might see only 4 categories when you look at your **Cloud Library screen**, but this screen is a carousel (moveable) screen and while 4 categories are listed, one of the listings is hidden.  **If you hold your finger down on this list and move your finger to left then to right on the screen,** you will find the carousel moves and another category appears.  While it appears to be 4 categories, it is really 5 categories.

At this point, you should have a good, fundamental base for operating the Amazon Music section.  If you will keep in mind the 3 major categories under which music is located:

- **Recent Activity**
- **Prime Music**
- **Library (Cloud Library)**

# 18. TV Streaming

Almost every TV station today has apps which you can download to see their station on streaming on this <u>Kindle Generation 5</u> ... CBS / NBC / FOX / ABC / ESPN / GOLF Channel / NFL / PBS and many more.

As you watch TV, watch for the **".com"** name of the station and how to download the TV station to watch on your Kindle.

Also I find the exact name of the app by typing the TV station into Google and asking for streaming information.

You will download an app (usually free) for your Kindle and when you have given the information concerning your TV provider, cable or satellite, you can install the app through Amazon by clicking a button instructing Amazon to install the app.  This allows you to receive the TV program that is streamed onto your Kindle.

As you order the free app from Amazon, you will need to know there is an app for a device call "Fire TV" stick.  This is a little confusing for we have

Kindle Fire units. But the Fire TV stick is a unit that attaches to your TV. **It is not the same as the Kindle Fire e-reader.**

So when you order an app like ESPN there are two versions: **ESPN WATCH** and ESPN Watch for Fire TV stick. **We need the ESPN WATCH.**

## Locating The Streamer

I was looking for a basketball game on **Fox Sports 1.** I went to Google and typed in Fox Sports 1 into the Google search. For Amazon Kindle, I found the name of the app is **Fox Sports Go** *(free app)*.

Then I went to the Amazon Shop. I typed **Fox Sports Go** into the search box at Amazon shop. And I clicked on the yellow search button on lower right side of my keyboard.

**A screen appeared showing streaming apps for several TV stations.**

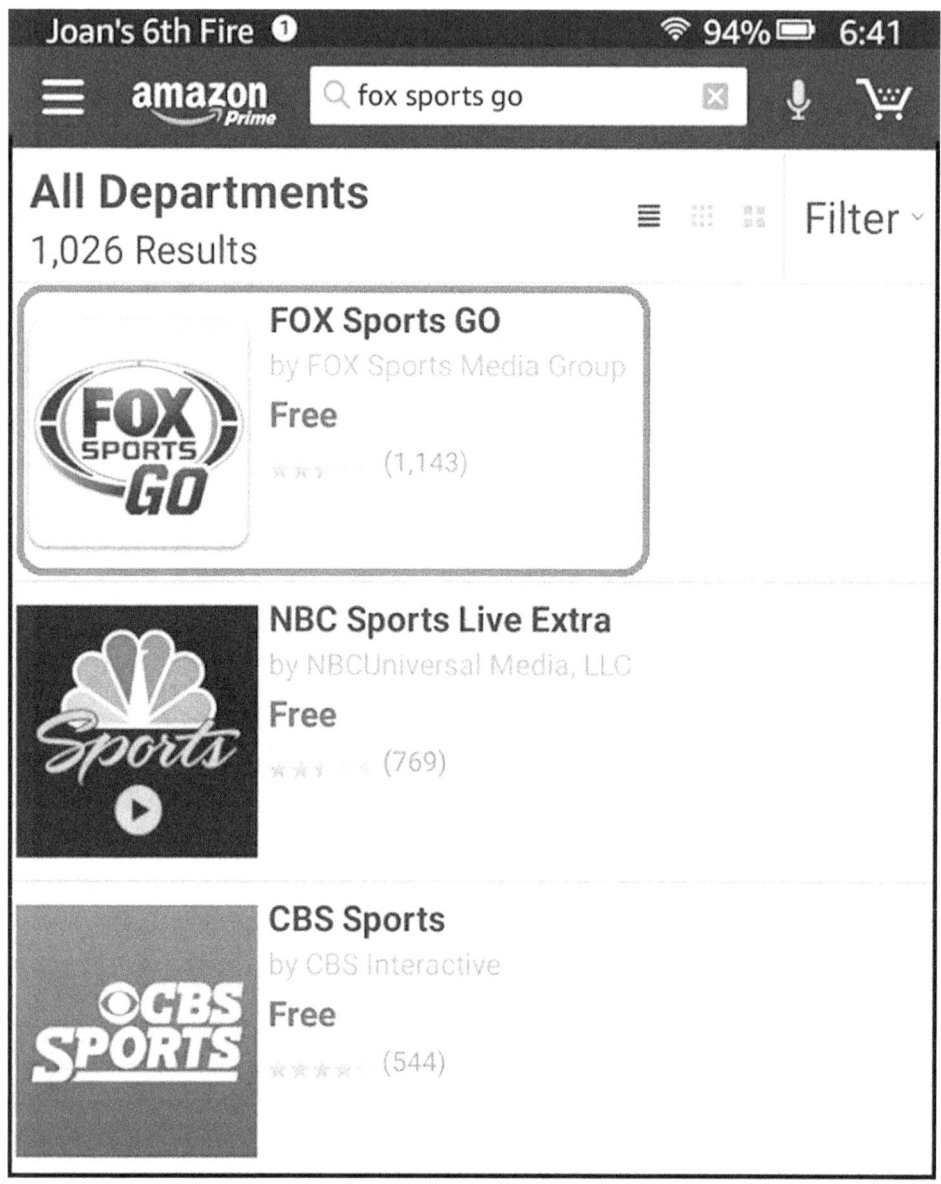

**Tap FOX Sports GO in the list.**

# To Obtain The App

On the page with Fox Sports Go, there was a Yellow box saying "Buy from Amazon Store" (Price is $0.00).

> Pam's second 8" Fire (5th gen) ❶    📶 37% 🔋 7:16
>
> ☰  amazon Prime    🔍 fox sports go    ⊠  🎤  🛒
>
> FOX SPORTS GO
>
> Price: $0.00
>
> Available instantly on your connected Android device.
>
> Buy from Amazon Appstore

## Tap on that Yellow Box.

The following screen comes up. Tap on the box saying **GET.**

When you see the following screen, tap on the box saying **DOWNLOAD.**

As it downloads and installs on your Kindle, you will often see a yellow line showing you the installation is in progress.

Another screen appears with a yellow box saying **OPEN**. Tap on that box.

It may ask you the name of your TV provider.

Tap on that.

**Your provider may require you to give your email address and password used with your provider.**

**When the required information is provided,**

**download should begin and in seconds you will have the app installed on your Kindle and the logo for the station will appear on your Home Page Icons.** *(The first time you watch the station you usually have to give this information. But in future watching, it is usually not requested. All you do the next time you watch is tap on the station icon on the Home Page.)*

**You will need to go through a registration procedure <u>for each station</u> the first time you watch that station.**

# 19. Camera

## Taking Pictures With Kindle Camera

A camera is built into the Kindle, and it is very easy to use.

**From the Home screen**, **tap on the Camera icon**.

There is a camera eye on the back of your Kindle in the top corner. On the screen you will see what is in front of the camera eye. **When using the Kindle as a camera, be careful to not cover the camera eye with your hand.**

By watching the screen as you move the Kindle, find what you would like for a picture.

**If you want to zoom in on an object in your picture**, put two fingers on the screen and move them apart. This causes the camera to zoom in on what is on the camera screen.

**When you are ready to take the picture ...**

**tap on the**  **symbol at the bottom of the screen.**

After you tap on  the picture you have taken shows up briefly (a second or two) on the screen, and then goes away.

**When finished taking pictures, you can get back to the Home screen** by swiping up from the bottom of the screen with your finger. The following shows up at the bottom of the screen. Tap the circle to go Home.

# Getting to the camera from the Cover screen

You can also bring up the camera from the Cover screen (the screen that comes up when you turn your Kindle on) ...

Put your finger on the camera symbol in the extreme bottom right corner of the Cover screen. Holding your finger on the screen, swipe to the left side of the screen.

On the screen you will see what is in front of the camera eye on the back top corner of your Kindle. **Be careful to not cover the camera eye with your hand.**

By watching what is on the screen, position your Kindle for the picture you want to take.

When you are ready to take the picture, **tap on the**  **symbol at the bottom of the screen**. The photo is taken.

When finished taking pictures, you can **get back to the Home screen** by swiping up from the bottom of the screen with your finger. The following shows up at the bottom of the screen.

**Tap the circle to go Home.**

# Using The Front-Facing Camera

In addition to the camera eye on the back top corner of your Kindle, there is also a camera eye on the front of your Kindle at the top center of the screen.

**From the Home screen**, **tap on the Camera icon**.

On the camera screen you will see what is in front of the camera eye on the back of your Kindle.

**To use the front-facing camera**, **tap on the symbol**  **at the top of the screen**.

**The front-facing camera is now activated.**

By watching what is on the screen, position your Kindle for the picture you want to take.

Tap on the  at the bottom of the screen to take the picture.

After the photo is taken, it will show up briefly (a second or two) on the screen, and then go away.

When finished taking pictures, you can **get back to the Home screen** by swiping up from the bottom of the screen with your finger. The following shows up at the bottom of the screen. Tap the circle to go Home.

## Camera Settings

There are a few camera settings that you may

want to consider when taking pictures.

From the Home screen tap on the Camera icon. The camera screen will come up.

**Tap on the**  **symbol** at the top right corner of the camera screen ...

The following settings screen comes up ...

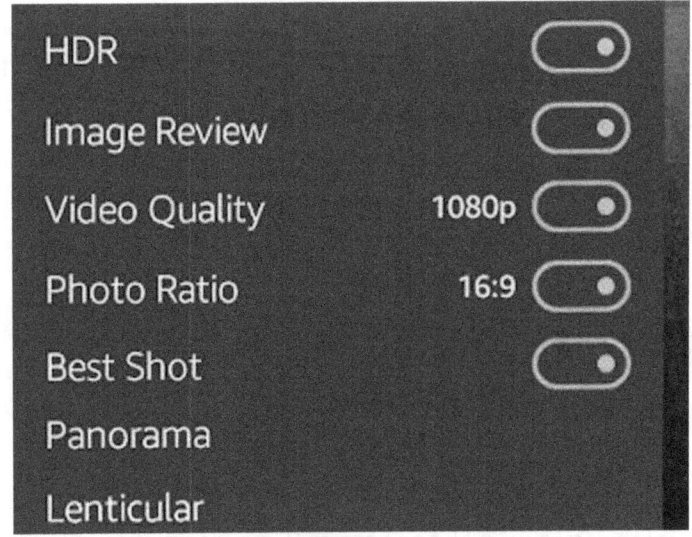

You can turn off and on the HDR (High Definition), Image Review, Video Quality, Photo ratio, and Best Shot switches with one tap on the 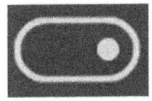 symbol.

By taking pictures after making adjustments to these switches, you will see the effect of each setting.

To return Home, swipe up from the bottom of the screen with your finger. Tap on the circle to go Home.

## Viewing Photos

To see your photos ... **from the Home screen tap on the Amazon Photos icon:**

A screen showing all your photos comes up. (If you do not see  ≡ **All**  in the top left corner of the screen, tap on the  ◁  symbol at the bottom of the screen. You may need to swipe up from the bottom of the screen to see this)

**<u>Tap on a picture</u>** and it will fill the screen.  To return to the screen with All your photos, tap on the ◁ symbol at the bottom of the screen.

**<u>Tap on the</u>** ⧉ **<u>symbol</u> in the top right area of the screen <u>to see a "slide show" of your photos</u>.**  One of your pictures will fill the screen for a few seconds, then the next picture will fill the screen for a few seconds, then the next, going through all of your pictures.

To return to the screen with All your photos, tap on the ◁ symbol at the bottom of the screen *(you may need to swipe up from the bottom of the screen to see this.)*

**Tap on the**  **symbol in the top right area of the screen to change the order the pictures are shown on the screen**.   The following screen comes up.  Tap on the option you want.

Date Taken   ✓

Date Uploaded

**Tap on the** **symbol** to create a new photo Album.

Enter the name you want for your album, then tap CREATE.  The album will be created.

Now you can put pictures in your album. **From the All photos screen, tap on a photo you want to put in the album**. The photo will fill the screen.

**Tap on the**  **symbol** at the top of the screen. A screen comes up showing the Albums you have created. **Tap on the name of the album you want to use for the photo**. The photo will be copied to this album.

To see your photo albums, put your finger on the left side of the screen and pull (swipe) toward the center of the screen. A narrow menu comes on the left-side of the screen.

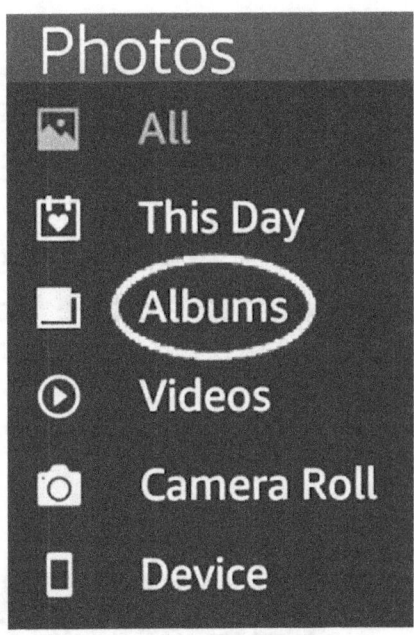

**Tap on Albums to see your albums.**

**Tap on the**  **symbol** in the top right area of the screen to activate the camera so you can take more pictures. Watch the screen to find what you want for a photo.

When you are ready to take the picture, tap on the symbol at the bottom of the screen.

When finished taking pictures, you can return to the All photos screen. **Tap on the** **symbol** at the bottom of the screen (You may need to swipe up from the bottom of the screen to see this symbol).

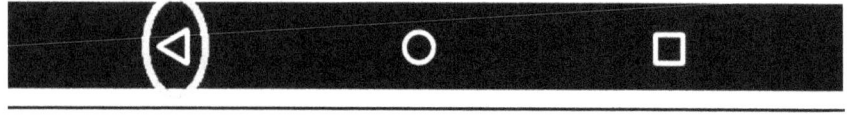

**When you are ready to leave the All photos screen**, **tap on the circle at the bottom of the screen to go to the Home screen**. You may need to swipe up from the bottom of the screen to see the circle.

# Editing A Photo

## From the Home screen tap on the Amazon Photos icon:

A screen showing all your photos comes up. (If you do not see ☰ All in the top left corner of the screen, tap on the ◁ symbol at the bottom of the screen. You may need to swipe up from the bottom of the screen to see this).

**Tap on the picture you want to edit** and it will fill the screen.

![screenshot of photo viewer showing a fluffy puppy]

**Tap on the**  **symbol** in the top right area of the screen.

Now at the bottom of the screen you will see several options you can use to make the picture look as you want.

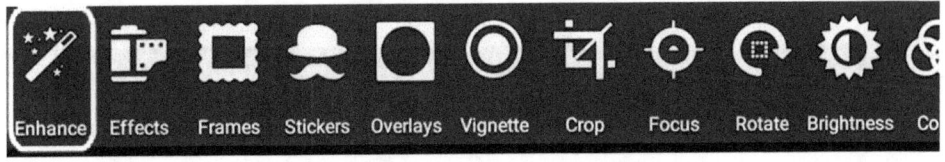

Scroll from right to left to see even more options. Tap on an option you want to try.

For example, you might **tap on Enhance**. Three options show up on the screen ...

Tap on each of these to see if you like the changes made to the picture.

**If you like the changes, tap on Apply** in the top right area of the screen. You can continue making other edits to the picture if you wish.

When you have finished editing the picture, you can save these changes. **Tap on Done** in the top right area of the screen.

If you do not want to save edits you have tried, tap on the  symbol at the bottom of the screen.

A box comes on screen asking you to confirm that you want to leave the editor without saving changes. **Tap on "LEAVE EDITOR"**.

**To return to the All photos screen, tap on the**  **symbol at the bottom of the screen**. You may need to swipe up from the bottom of the screen to see this symbol.

## Email Photos

From the Home Page, **tap on the on Amazon Photos icon**.

A screen showing all your photos comes up. *(If you do not see* ≡ **All** *in the top left corner of the screen, tap on the* ◁ *symbol at the bottom of the screen. You may need to swipe up from the bottom of the screen to see this)*

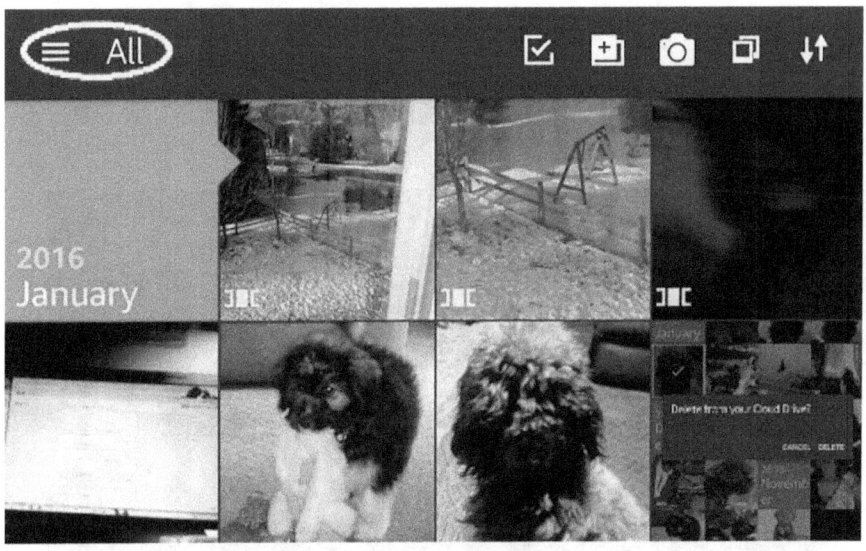

From the composite of photos shown **tap the photo you want to send.**

The photo will appear on the full screen.

At the top of the screen you'll see:

**Tap on the** <image src="share symbol" /> **symbol.**

A screen displays with a list of applications.

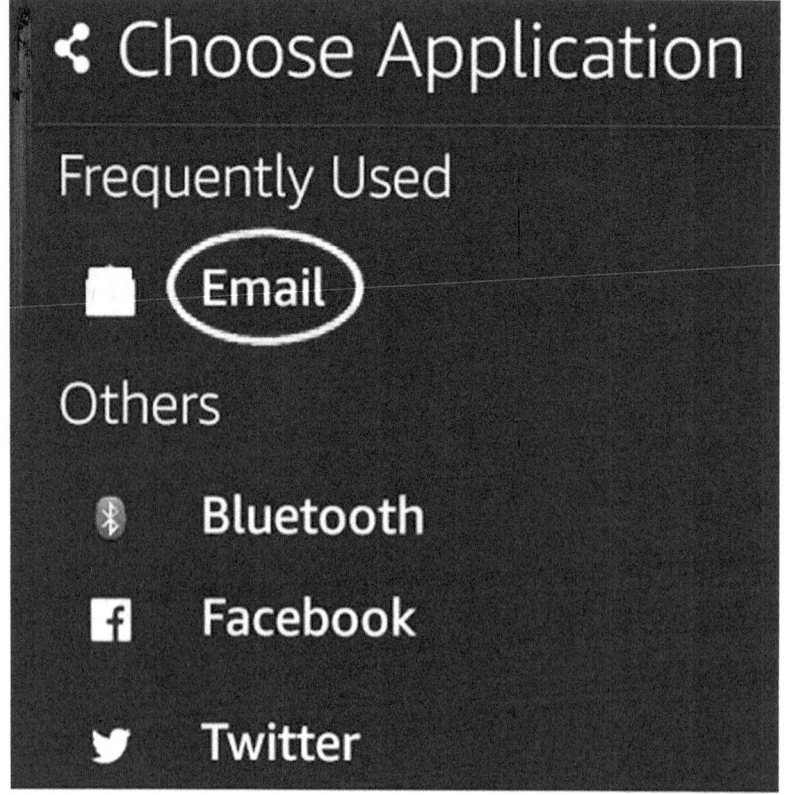

**Tap on Email.**

An email screen will come up with the picture on it ...

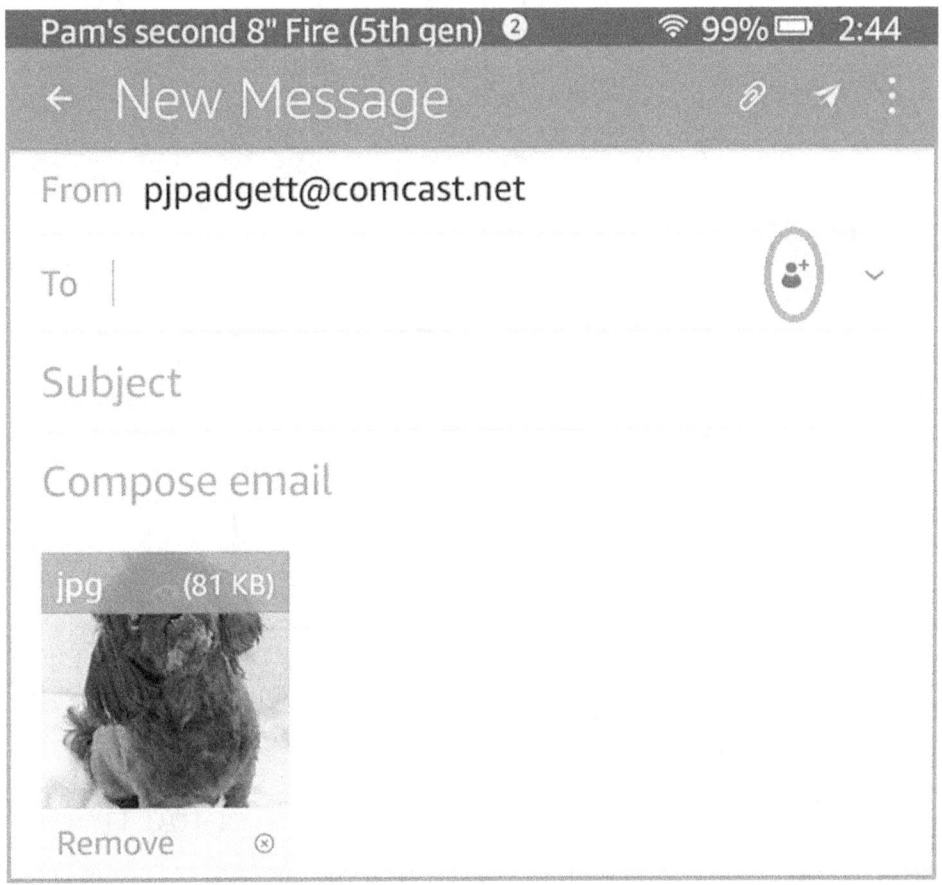

You may enter the email address of the person you want to receive this email, or you may choose that person from your Contacts.

To choose the person from your Contacts, tap on the 🧑⁺ symbol. Your contact list will be shown. Tap on whichever contact you want.

If you want to send more than one photo, tap on the paperclip at top right corner of the screen:

A small screen comes up.

Attach a Photo

Attach a File

Capture a Photo

**Tap on Attach a Photo**

The screen with all your photos will come up again.  Tap on another photo you want to send in the email.

When you have attached each photo you want to send in the email, and typed any message in the "Compose email" area of the email screen,  you're ready to send the email.

Tap on the paper airplane at the top of the email screen:

**Your photo has been sent!**

To exit photo and return to Home Page, tap the circle at bottom of Kindle screen.

## Deleting Photos

Photos you have taken can be deleted from your Kindle with the following steps:

From the Home screen, **tap on the Photos icon:**

A screen showing all your photos comes up. (If you do not see ≡ All in the top left corner of the screen, tap on the ◁ symbol at the bottom of the screen. You may need to swipe up from the bottom of the screen to see this)

**Tap on a photo you want to delete.** The photo will be shown in the full screen.

In the top right corner of the screen tap on the  symbol. *(garbage can)*

A screen asking you to confirm that you want to delete this photo comes on screen.

When photos are taken with the camera they are saved on your Kindle and on "the Cloud Drive", a place Amazon provides for us to store such things as photos. The Kindle must have a wi-fi connection to store or delete the photos on the

Cloud Drive.

**Check the box "Also delete from your Cloud Drive"** for photos you do not want to save at all. This will cause the photo to be deleted from both your Kindle and the Cloud Drive. **You will no longer see that photo on your screen of pictures.**

**Do not check the box "Also delete from your Cloud Drive"** if you want to delete a photo from your Kindle to free up storage space, but still keep the photo on the Cloud Drive. **As long as the photo is on the Cloud Drive, you will see it on your screen of photos.**

**Tap on Delete** to confirm deleting the photo.

# 20. Screen Prints: Reproduction of Kindle Screen

## Create A Screen Print

You can take a picture of the screen you see on the Kindle.

Go to the screen to be photographed.

**Press the silver bar that <u>lowers</u> volume** *(the left-most silver bar)* **<u>&</u> the <u>On/Off bar</u>** *(silver bar right side)* **at the same time.**

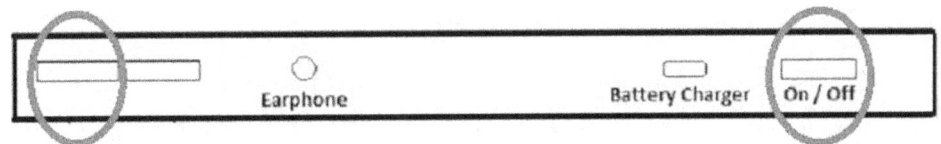

**Release both bars after a slight "flash" occurs on screen and the photo in a partial, but narrow size, appears briefly on screen.**

*(You'll see what looks like a snapshot of what you have on the Kindle screen pop up for just a second, then go away.)*

You now have a photo of that Kindle screen.

The picture of the Kindle screen can be seen just as any other photo. **From the Home screen tap on the Amazon Photos icon.**

A screen showing **all your photos** comes up.

## Email A Screen Print

After you make a screen print, you can email the screen print and even write a message along with the photo of the screen print.

From Home Page, tap on **Photos**. After all photos appear on screen, tap on the photo of the Screen Print. After the screen print photo appears on full screen, **tap on the share symbol on top right of screen.**

A screen displays with a list of applications.

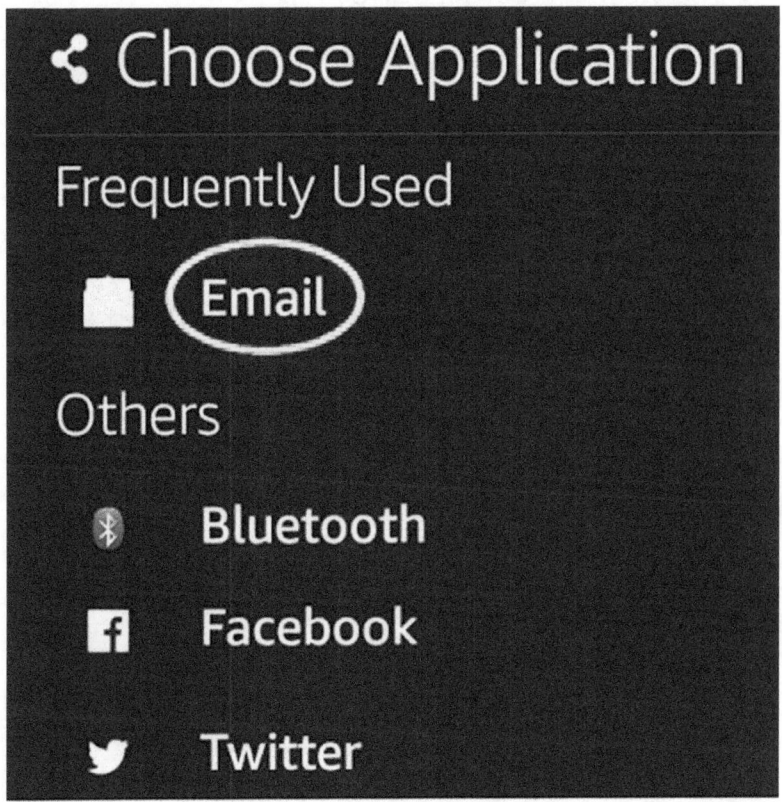

**Tap on Email.**

An email screen will come up with the picture on it ...

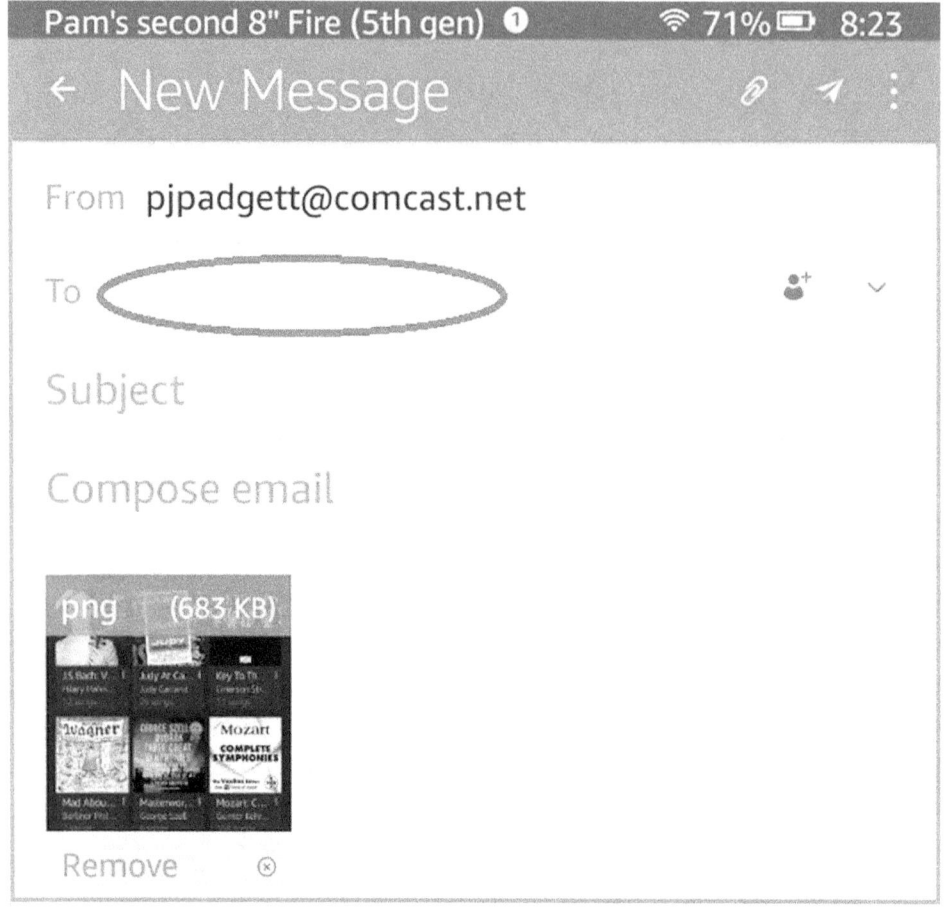

Type into the email **"To"** the first letters of the name of the person you want to email. As long as that person is in your Contacts, the email address will appear on screen. Tap on name of that person.

Type message if you care to do so in **"Compose Email"**.

Tap the **"Send"** icon at top right of screen ... the **"paper airplane"** symbol.

# 21. Microphone: Dictation On Kindle

A fun part of the Kindle Fire Generation 5 is the voice recognition program which allows you to dictate emails by voice or to use your voice for the machine to type in search box when you go to Kindle shop.

Any time the microphone appears on the Kindle screen at the bottom of the keyboard, you have the option to record your typing by speaking the words you want typed.

Just tap on the microphone symbol, to the left of the space bar, on the keyboard.

The keyboard will disappear and a microphone will appear in its place.

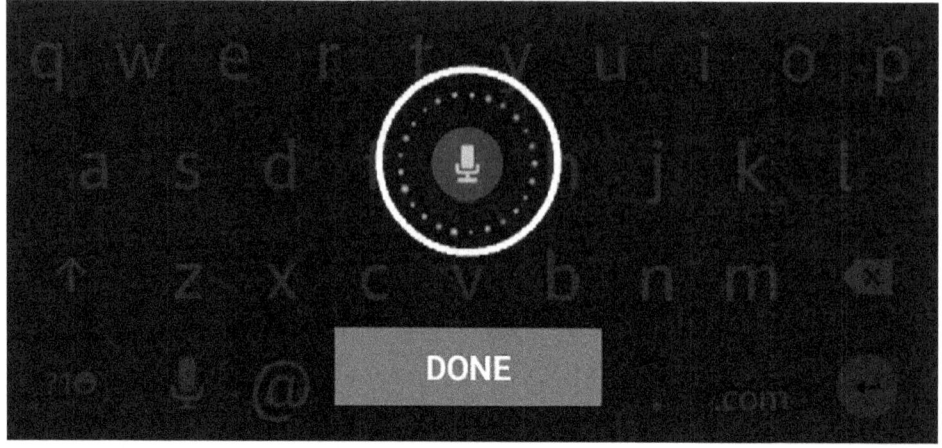

**Begin speaking in a normal voice.**

**After you speak, the words spoken will appear typed on the email or in the search box.**

If you pause and do not speak for a few minutes, the keyboard will return and **the microphone pictured in the above graphic** will disappear.

You can resume voice dictation any time by one tap on the microphone at bottom left of keyboard.

**It is fun to use. Don't hesitate to practice by dictating to an email or search box. You can always delete what you record (type).**

You will likely find that the device doesn't recognize some of your vocal accents or enunciation. A few very strange words often appear when this is the case. Don't worry. You can correct those errors by using your keyboard. Just backspace over the typed letters which you want to remove.

I use this dictation program a lot when I am writing emails. I'm learning to speak "**new paragraph**" and "**period**" and "**comma**" to the machine and it is beginning to feel more natural to me.

## Practice Using The Microphone

We encourage you to practice using the microphone by putting your own email address on your contact list and dictating an email using the microphone.

You can take this section of writing (or any writing) and read it into the microphone on the email to yourself.

This is a great way to learn to use the microphone and also to learn sending emails.

# 22. Rebooting ... Correcting Problems

On the **right side / top edge ...** of Kindle ... is **a single <u>silver bar</u>** where you turn Kindle on and off.

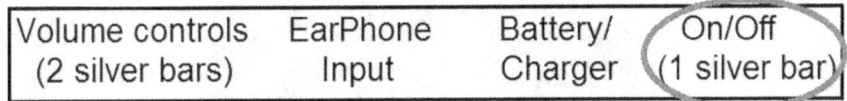

**To "reboot" Kindle, press <u>and hold down</u>** *the silver power bar* **until the following comes on screen:**

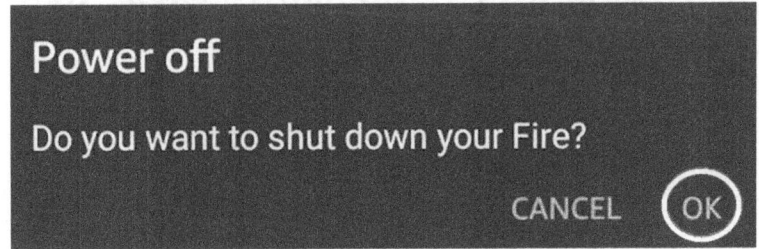

**Tap "<u>OK</u>"**

Screen will go black.

**Wait about 20 seconds**

Then **press the silver power bar** and <u>**hold the bar down with your finger**</u> until "Amazon" appears center screen ... <u>**then release finger**</u> from power bar.

The unit is reloading / the word <u>**"Fire"**</u> will appear ...

A few seconds later the standard "cover page" with the lock at bottom center, will appear on screen.

**<u>Unlock</u>** by **<u>swiping</u>** upward from bottom of screen where the lock icon is located.

*(**To swipe**: place finger on the "lock" icon, located on bottom of screen. ... <u>hold finger down </u>while moving finger to top of screen)*

**Home page will appear on screen.**

Kindle is now re-booted and ready for normal use.

*(At end of day **<u>when you finish using Kindle,</u>** before you plug in the electrical line to re-charge battery, it is recommended that you shut down the Kindle and reboot the next morning as you remove the battery charge line.)*

Rebooting is a standard method used with electrical systems to clean out the system and refresh the units.  It is used with sound equipment, with satellite boxes, with computers, and with Kindle.

If you have difficulty with your units, it is one of the first things to try in restoring unit.

# 23. Removing Advertisements

Advertisements will display on the "lock screen" (cover page) of your Kindle Fire unless you **unsubscribe** to the ads.  There is a $15 charge to unsubscribe to the ads.

If you ordered your Kindle directly form Amazon, you may have unsubscribed to the ads, and paid the additional $15, at that time.  Otherwise you can unsubscribe from the ads at any time with the following steps:

From the Home screen, tap on the Silk Browser icon:

Near the top of the screen is a long gray box.  **Tap in that box and type amazon.com**.

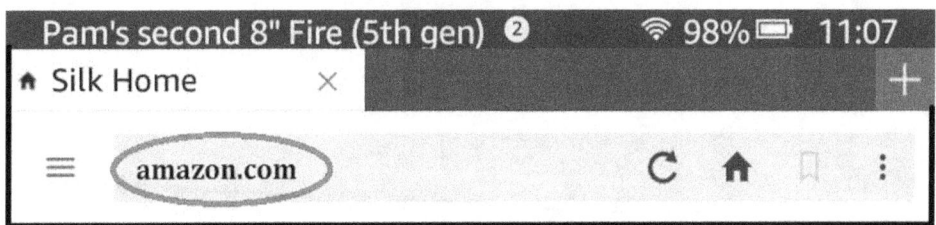

The Amazon website comes on screen. In the **top right area of the screen** you'll see **Your Account**.

**Tap on Your Account.**

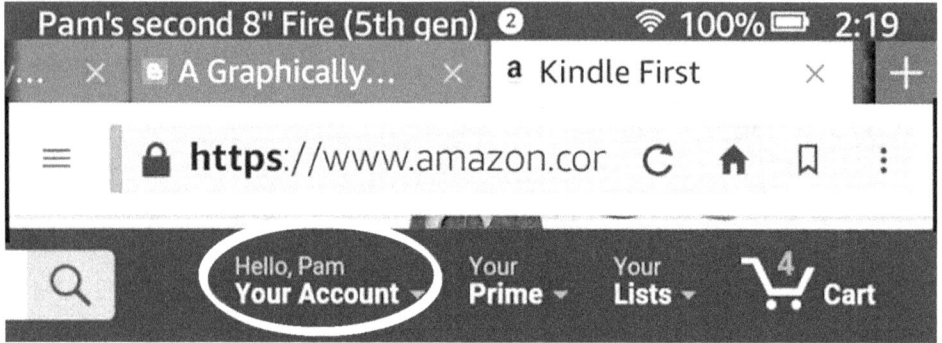

*(A narrow box may come on screen with a list of items. <u>If you see this</u>, tap on the first item, **Your Account**, in this list.)*

On the screen that comes up, **scroll down to the area titled <u>Digital Content</u>**. Tap on **Manage your Content and Devices.**

| Digital Content | Digital Management |
|---|---|
| Video, Music & Downloads | Manage Your Content and Devices |
| | Manage Your Cloud Subscriptions |
| | Your Video Subscriptions |
| | Your Amazon Music Settings |
| | Your Video Library |
| | Your Watchlist |
| | Your Games and Software Library |
| | Digital Gifts You Have Received |
| | Your Apps and Devices |
| | Amazon Instant Video Settings |

If the Amazon login screen displays again, you will need to type in your password and tap on **Sign in**.

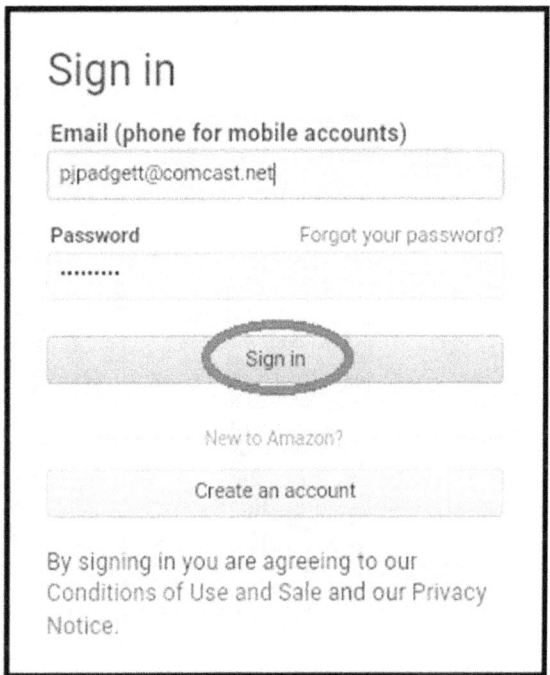

The screen for managing your content and devices comes up.

**Tap on the "Your Devices" tab.**

You'll see each device (such as a Kindle) you have registered with Amazon ...

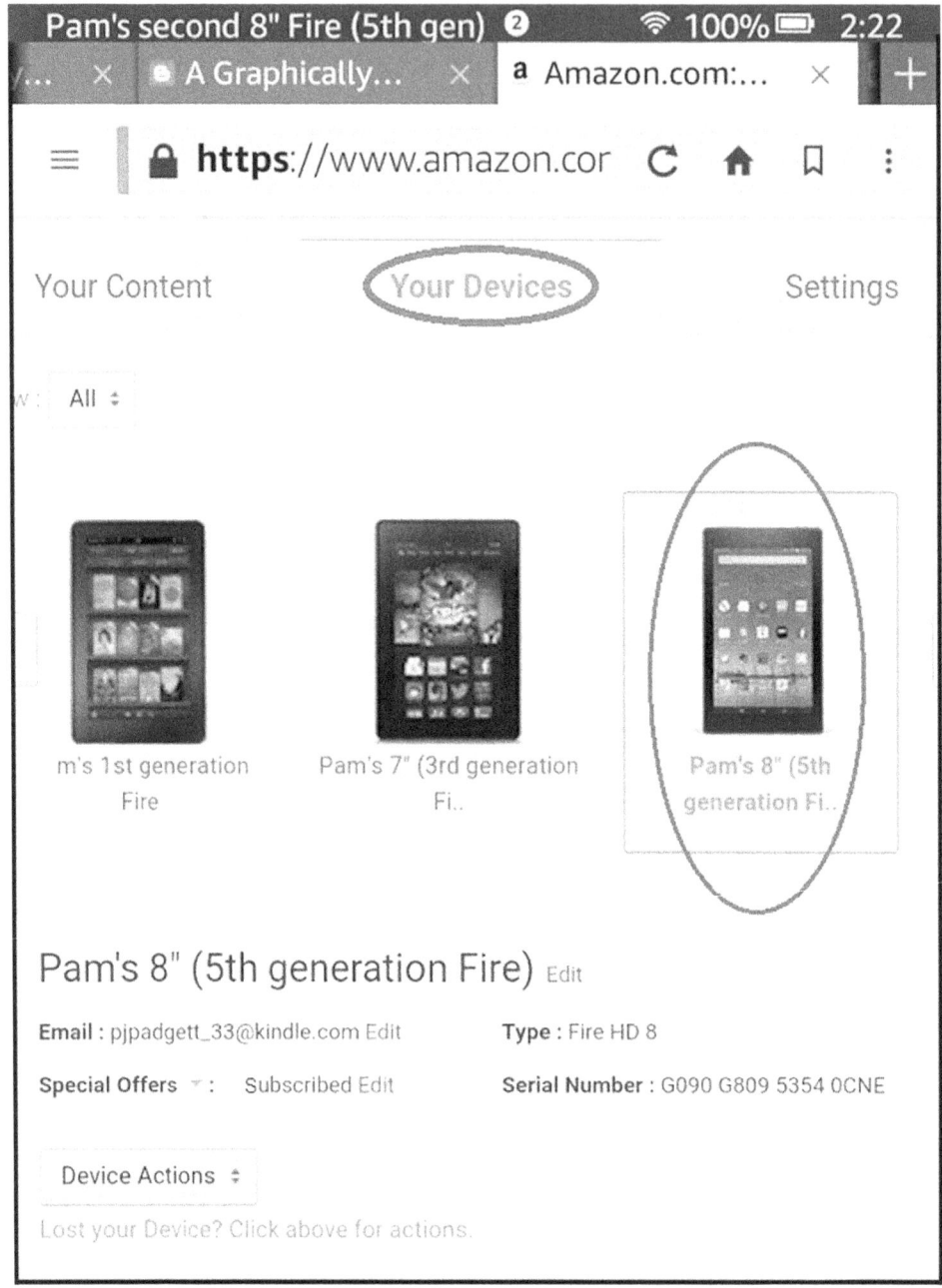

**Tap on the Kindle with ads you want to remove**. A lightly-colored box will be around that Kindle when it is selected.

Under the pictures you'll see information about that Kindle. Next to **Special Offers** you'll see the word **Subscribed** followed by **Edit.**

**Tap on Edit** next to Subscribed.

A popup screen displays explaining that you'll be charged **(a one-time fee)** $15 plus tax to unsubscribe for ads.

Tap on the yellow box **"Unsubscribe now with 1-Click"**

A confirmation screen displays. **Tap** on **OK.**

Amazon will send an email confirming that the subscription to ads has been cancelled and gives the amount charged to your account to do this.

*(A few minutes later I looked at my kindle and the ads were gone. I also re-booted my Kindle.)*

# 24. Deregistering Kindle

During setup of your Kindle you registered it with Amazon. If you want to register your Kindle to another Amazon account, or plan to return the Kindle, you can deregister it.

**If you still have the Kindle**, you can deregister it as follows:

From the **Home Page**, tap on the **Settings** icon:

On the Settings screen scroll to the area labels "**Personal**" and tap on **My Account** ...

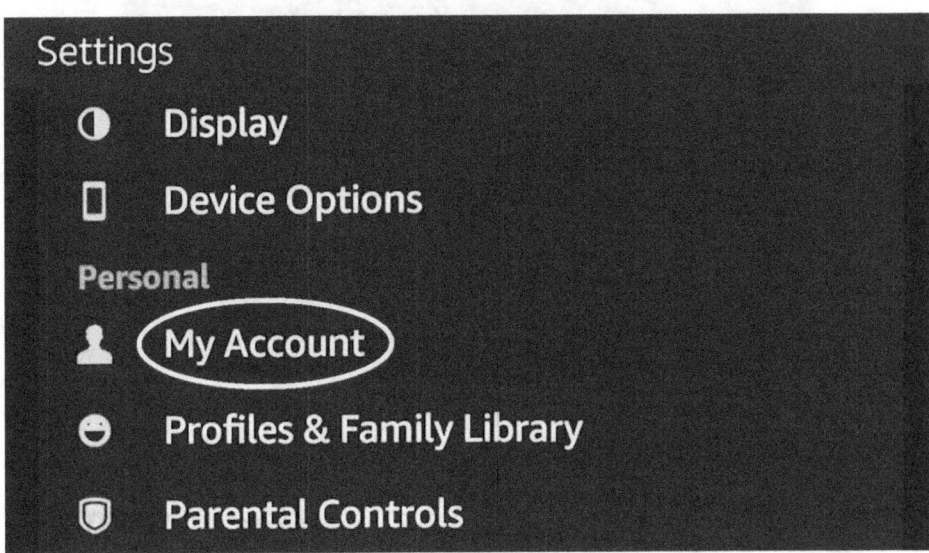

On the My Account screen, tap on **Deregister** ...

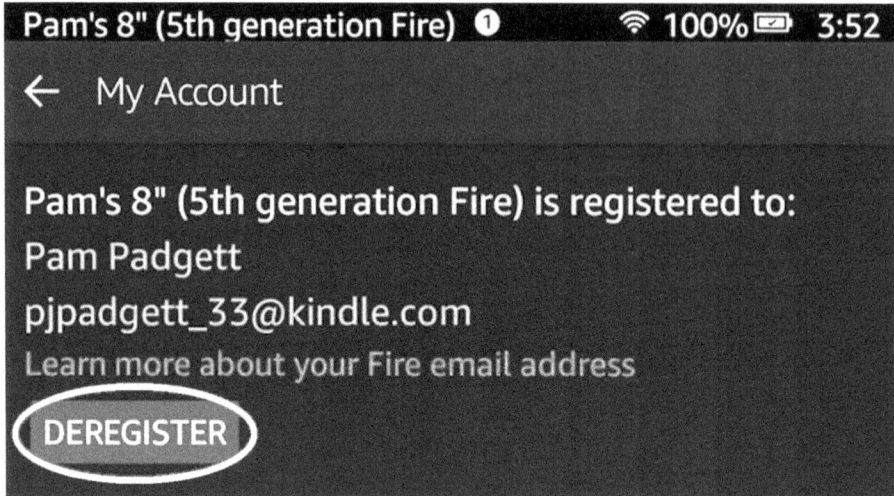

A confirmation screen comes up ....

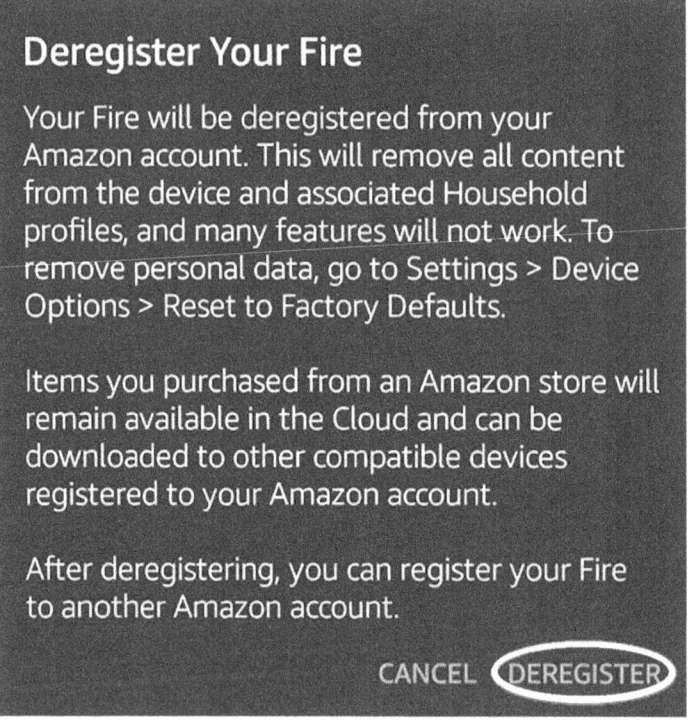

**To complete the deregistering, tap on DEREGISTER at the bottom of the screen.**

**If you no longer have the Kindle**, you can deregister it from another computer. Go to amazon.com.

In the top right corner of the Amazon.com screen, you'll see **Your Account**...

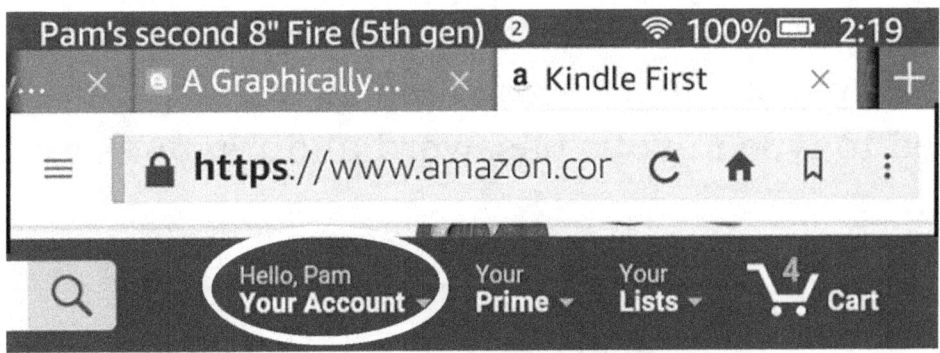

**Tap on Your Account in the top right area of the screen.** *(A narrow box may come on screen with a list of items. If you see this, tap on the first item, **Your Account**, in this list.)*

On the screen that comes up, **scroll down to the area title Digital Content.**

| Digital Content | Digital Management |
|---|---|
| Video, Music & Downloads | Manage Your Content and Devices |
| | Manage Your Cloud Subscriptions |
| | Your Video Subscriptions |
| | Your Amazon Music Settings |
| | Your Video Library |
| | Your Watchlist |
| | Your Games and Software Library |
| | Digital Gifts You Have Received |
| | Your Apps and Devices |
| | Amazon Instant Video Settings |

## Tap on Manage your Content and Devices.

If the Amazon login screen displays again, you will need to type in your password and tap on **Sign in...**.

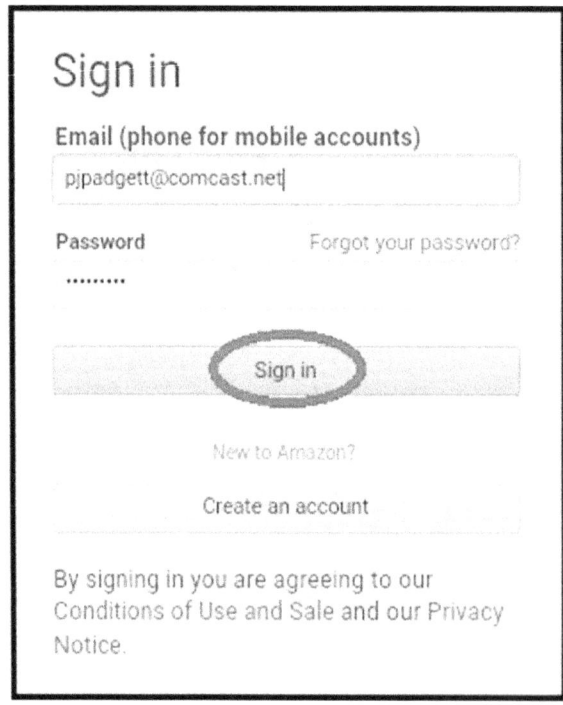

The screen for managing your content and devices comes up. **Tap on the "Your Devices" tab.**

A screen shows each device (such as a Kindle) you have registered with Amazon.

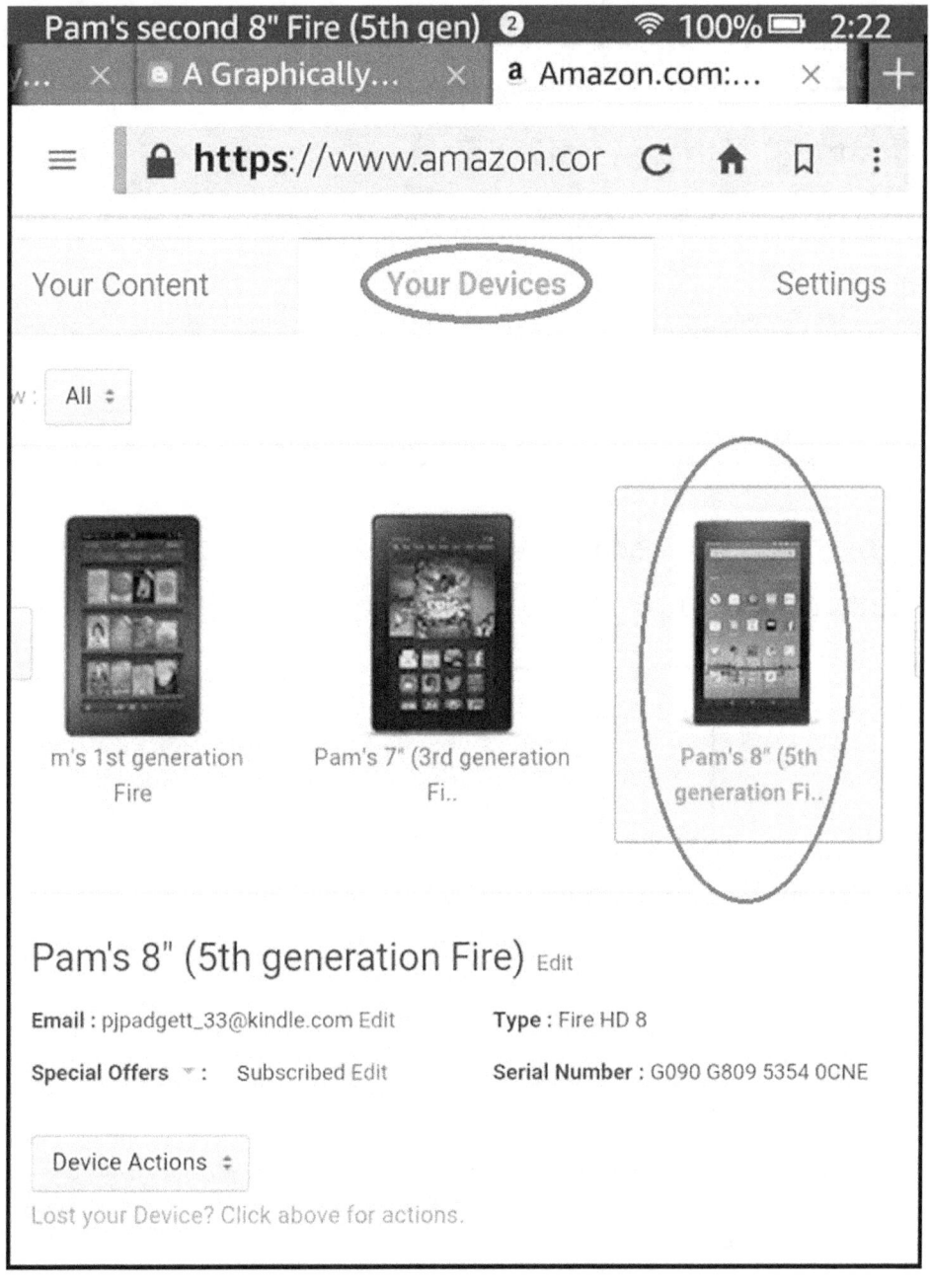

**Tap on the Kindle you want to deregister**. A lightly-colored box will be around that Kindle when it is selected.

Information about the selected device displays under the area with the pictures. There is also a button that says **"Device Actions"**.

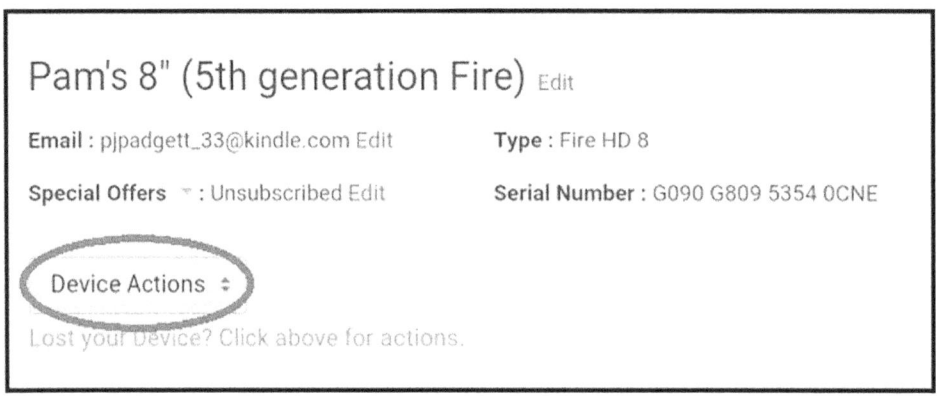

**Tap on Device Actions button**. A box comes up under the Device Actions button ...

> Deregister
>
> Set as default device
>
> Manage Firefly image and audio
>
> Remote Alarm
>
> Find Your Tablet
>
> Remote Lock
>
> Remote Factory Reset
>
> Warranty Service Center

**Tap on Deregister.**

## The following screen comes up ...

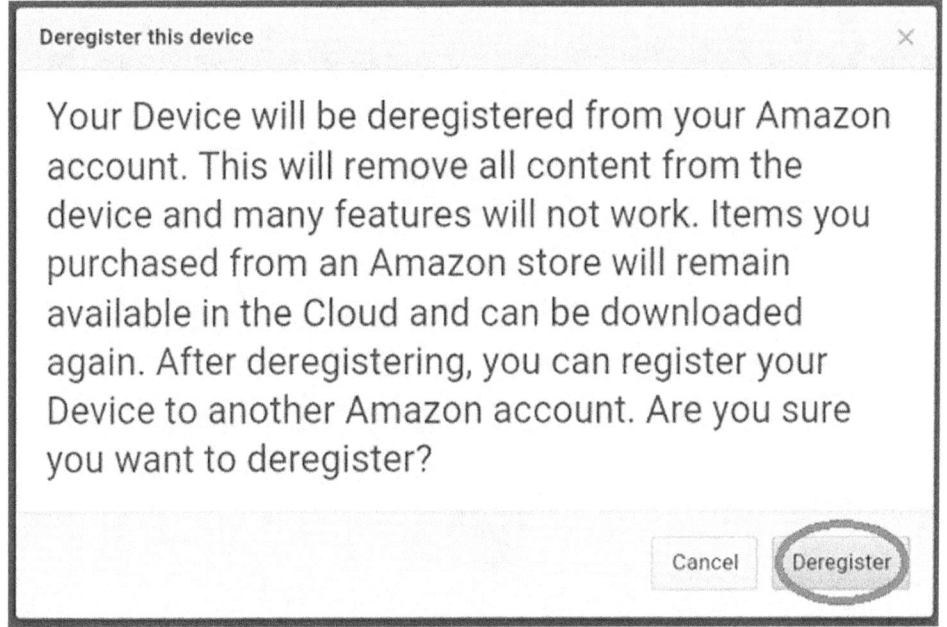

## Tap the yellow "Deregister" button.

A message displays that the device is in queue to be deregistered, and there is no longer a picture for that device on the screen.

# A Lighter Touch for Animal Lovers

...

Pam's 8" (5th generation Fire)  ●  🛜 64% 🔋 2:53

← Edit contact  🗑  ⋮

👤 Calley Boney ⌄

(phonetic name) Calley! ⌄

(nickname) NO! Don't Hiss At Me ...

📷  CHANGE

📞 1-000-000-0000  Mobile ▾ ✕

✉ calleyboney@comcast.netHome ▾ ✕

(email) doesn't read well  Work ▾ ✕

📍 (address) varies,  Home ▾
   especially at night  ✕

🏢 Domestic Worker
   ✕
(title) Chief Mouser

💬 (notes) Approach with caution ... best
   to have broom in your hand when
   going near her.  (might also put  ✕
   Neosporin and band-aids nearby)

255

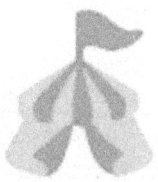

## Menagerie

A strange or diverse collection of animals

A collection of wild animals kept in captivity for exhibition

Pretty Girl ...

Intruder!

# The End

# Special Treats ... Rebooting humans ...

Did you want something?

ZZZZZ ....

Maggie

Look what
I just did ...

(previous dog bed)

# Resting

## "Cat Warmers"
## ($50,000 Mark Levinson amplifiers)

*In August, 2015, a momma calico cat and her 3 kittens moved into my courtyard! The kittens were completely wild. The momma kept trying to attack me. (see picture of Calley)*

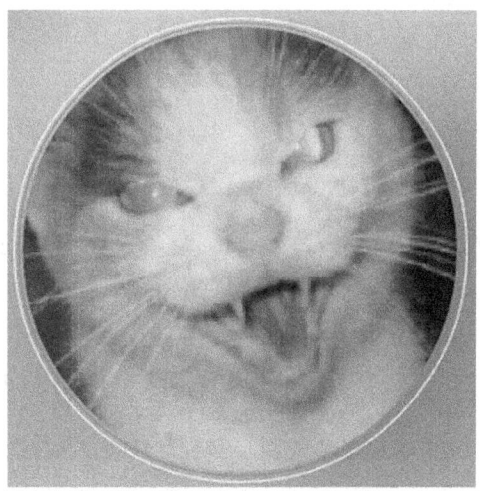

# Calley

*I tried to get help from animal control without having the cats destroyed but that would not be possible so I decided these cats could live in my courtyard and I would feed them and give them water.*

*As winter approached I decided to buy a dog house for these cats.*

*I found a dog house on Internet and called to order it. A young man, probably from India, took my order.*

*At the end of the order, he said: "Would you like to buy a large bag of dog bones for your dog?"*

*I replied: "I don't have a dog."*

*There was a moment of silence...*

*Then he said:  "OHhhhhh... Kay."*

*When he recovered, I told him I bought the dog house for a momma cat and her 3 kittens who moved into my courtyard ... (I'm not certain he ever heard me.)*

*Winter arrived, and I think they (the 4 cats) chose to live in the dog house at night when weather was cold.  I had a man fix a smaller door on the house so not as much weather could get into the door.  (I changed the dog door into cat door.)*

*They are all still here and I still feed them daily ... sometimes both morning and evenings... They are very fat now!*

# More ...

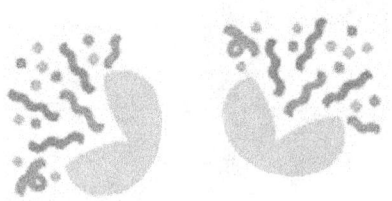

# A sweetheart
## Lucy

## School Days!

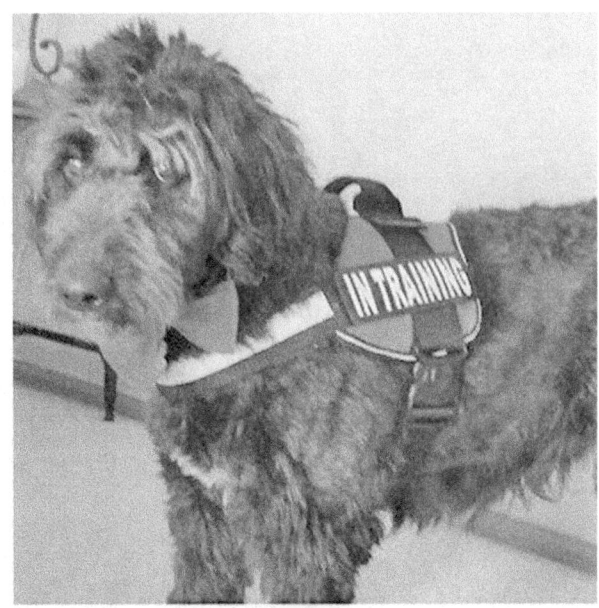

**Gus**

**Gracie**

Patches

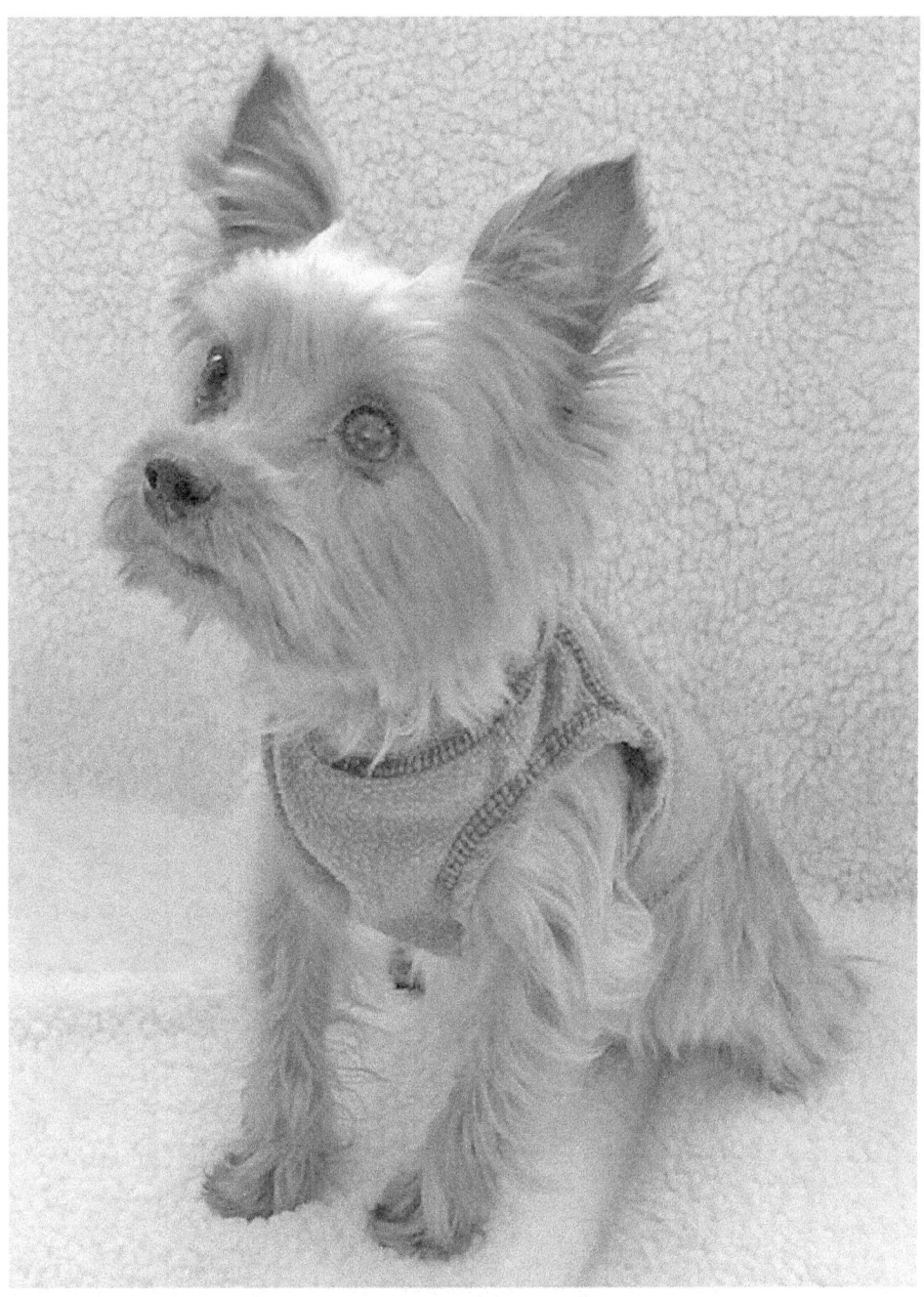

**Bodhi**

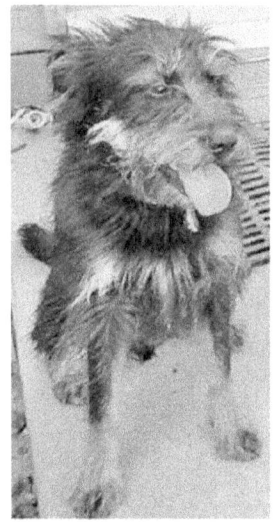

Scout

Zoomie

Chewey

# Sweet Sadie

**Tallulah ... *(alias ... "cat")***

www.ingramcontent.com/pod-product-compliance
Lightning Source LLC
Chambersburg PA
CBHW080651190526
45169CB00006B/2069